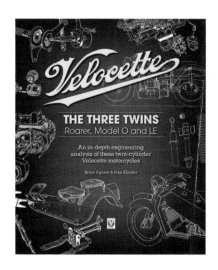

Dedicated to Grahame and Adrian, who put
so much effort into restoring the Roarer

More motorcycle books from Veloce Publishing

BMW Boxer Twins 1970-1995 Bible, The (Falloon)
BMW Cafe Racers (Cloesen)
BMW Custom Motorcycles – Choppers, Cruisers, Bobbers, Trikes & Quads (Cloesen)
British Café Racers (Cloesen)
British Custom Motorcycles – The Brit Chop – choppers, cruisers, bobbers & trikes (Cloesen)
Bonjour – Is this Italy? (Turner)
British 250cc Racing Motorcycles (Pereira)
BSA Bantam Bible, The (Henshaw)
BSA Motorcycles – the final evolution (Jones)
Ducati 750 Bible, The (Falloon)
Ducati 750 SS 'round-case' 1974, The Book of the (Falloon)
Ducati 860, 900 and Mille Bible, The (Falloon)
Ducati Monster Bible (New Updated & Revised Edition), The (Falloon)
Ducati Story, The – 6th Edition (Falloon)
Ducati 916 (updated edition) (Falloon)
Fine Art of the Motorcycle Engine, The (Peirce)
Franklin's Indians (Sucher/Pickering/Diamond/Havelin)
From Crystal Palace to Red Square – A Hapless Biker's Road to Russia (Turner)
Funky Mopeds (Skelton)
India - The Shimmering Dream (Reisch/Falls (translator))
Italian Cafe Racers (Cloesen)
Italian Custom Motorcycles (Cloesen)
Japanese Custom Motorcycles – The Nippon Chop – Chopper, Cruiser, Bobber, Trikes and Quads (Cloesen)
Kawasaki Triples Bible, The (Walker)
Kawasaki W, H1 & Z – The Big Air-cooled Machines (Long)
Kawasaki Z1 Story, The (Sheehan)
Lambretta Bible, The (Davies)
Laverda Twins & Triples Bible 1968-1986 (Falloon)
Little book of trikes, the (Quellin)
Moto Guzzi Sport & Le Mans Bible, The (Falloon)
Moto Guzzi Story, The – 3rd Edition (Falloon)
Motorcycle Apprentice (Cakebread)
Motorcycle GP Racing in the 1960s (Pereira)
Motorcycle Racing with the Continental Circus 1920-1970 (Pereira)

Motorcycle Road & Racing Chassis Designs (Noakes)
Motorcycles and Motorcycling in the USSR from 1939 (Turbett)
Motorcycling in the '50s (Clew)
MV Agusta Fours, The book of the classic (Falloon)
MV Agusta since 1945 (Falloon)
Norton Commando Bible – All models 1968 to 1978 (Henshaw)
Off-Road Giants! (Volume 1) – Heroes of 1960s Motorcycle Sport (Westlake)
Off-Road Giants! (Volume 2) – Heroes of 1960s Motorcycle Sport (Westlake)
Off-Road Giants! (Volume 3) – Heroes of 1960s Motorcycle Sport (Westlake)
Peking to Paris 2007 (Young)
Racing Classic Motorcycles (Reynolds)
Racing Line – British motorcycle racing in the golden age of the big single (Guntrip)
The Red Baron's Ultimate Ducati Desmo Manual (Cabrera Choclán)
Scooters & Microcars, The A-Z of Popular (Dan)
Scooter Lifestyle (Grainger)
Scooter Mania! – Recollections of the Isle of Man International Scooter Rally (Jackson)
Slow Burn - The growth of Superbikes & Superbike racing 1970 to 1988 (Guntrip)
Suzuki Motorcycles - The Classic Two-stroke Era (Long)
Triumph Bonneville Bible (59-83) (Henshaw)
Triumph Bonneville!, Save the – The inside story of the Meriden Workers' Co-op (Rosamond)
Triumph Motorcycles & the Meriden Factory (Hancox)
Triumph Speed Twin & Thunderbird Bible (Woolridge)
Triumph Tiger Cub Bible (Estall)
Triumph Trophy Bible (Woolridge)
TT Talking – The TT's most exciting era – As seen by Manx Radio TT's lead commentator 2004-2012 (Lambert)
Velocette Motorcycles – MSS to Thruxton – Third Edition (Burris)
Vespa – The Story of a Cult Classic in Pictures (Uhlig)
Vincent Motorcycles: The Untold Story since 1946 (Guyony & Parker)

www.veloce.co.uk

First published in May 2023 by Veloce Publishing Limited, Veloce House, Parkway Farm Business Park, Middle Farm Way, Poundbury, Dorchester DT1 3AR, England. Tel +44 (0)1305 260068 / Fax 01305 250479 / e-mail info@veloce.co.uk / web www.veloce.co.uk or www.velocebooks.com. ISBN: 978-1-787119-00-0; UPC: 6-36847-01900-6.
Readers with ideas for automotive books, or books on other transport or related hobby subjects, are invited to write to the editorial director of Veloce Publishing at the above address.
British Library Cataloguing in Publication Data – A catalogue record for this book is available from the British Library. Typesetting, design and page make-up all by Veloce Publishing Ltd on Apple Mac. Printed in India by Replika Press.

THE THREE TWINS
Roarer, Model O and LE

Brian Agnew & Ivan Rhodes

VELOCE PUBLISHING
THE PUBLISHER OF FINE AUTOMOTIVE BOOKS

Contents

About the authors

Brian's collection of LE-derived bikes.

Brian Agnew is Emeritus Professor of Energy and the Environment at Northumbria University, and a Visiting Professor to NewRail at Newcastle University. He was a European Engineer, Chartered Engineer, and Fellow of the Institution of Mechanical Engineers prior to retirement.

Brian studied mechanical engineering at Brunel University whilst sponsored by Rolls-Royce, Derby, and subsequently studied for a Masters degree in Internal Combustion Engineering at Kings College, London, followed by a PhD at City University, London that examined exhaust emission formation in spark ignition engines. It was whilst working at Rolls-Royce Derby in the 1960s that Brian met Ivan at Borrowash, establishing a lifelong friendship with Ivan and his sons, Grahame and Adrian, and an interest in Velocette motorcycles.

Ivan Rhodes is well known in the motorcycle fraternity as the authority on Velocette motorcycles. He served his apprenticeship as a motorcycle fitter at Wileman's Motors in Derby, and engaged in motorcycle racing at the Isle of Man TT and in the vintage motorcycle scene. Ivan was active for many years in the racing section of the Vintage Motorcycle Club, where he performed very well on his Velocettes.

Over the years, Ivan has put together an impressive and unique collection of Velocette and Wolverhampton AJS motorcycles that includes the Roarer and the Model O Velocettes. He is president of the Velocette Owners Club, and

often makes contributions to the club magazine, *Fishtail*, and is also the author of *Technical Excellence Exemplified* and *Passion of a Life Time*, both comprehensive accounts of Velocette single cylinder motorcycles.

Right: Ivan in his workshop.
Below: Ivan at the Isle of Man parade.

Acknowledgements

The majority of the pictures and illustrations come from the collections of Ivan Rhodes and from the LE Velo Club archives; the remainder are mainly from Brian's collection, though there are a small number from Mortons Media Group Ltd that are reproduced with permission. The authors thank John Rogerson for his help in proof reading, Kenneth Mitchell for helping with the pictures and for his thoughtful suggestions, and the LE Velo Club; in particular, Colin Roberts (editor of *On The Level,* the LE Club magazine), and Charles Phillips (Technical Secretary, LE Club) for their assistance in bringing this work to fruition.

Special thanks go to David Holder of The Velocette Motorcycle Company for permission to use the Velocette name and logo.

The Roarer at Fellside, Ivan's house in Borrowash, Derby.

Preface

To many motorcycle enthusiasts the Velocette represents the pinnacle of achievement in the design and performance of the single cylinder motorcycle. For 25 years from 1926 Veloce produced a range of world-beating, single cylinder, overhead camshaft (OHC) 350cc motorcycles that won several Junior Tourist Trophy races (TTs), many continental Grands Prix, and two world championships in the hands of Freddie Frith and Bob Foster. Veloce produced factory specials for the works teams that were used to develop the first TT replica machines that could be bought by motorcycle enthusiasts. Such was the quality of these machines that, on several occasions, Velocette machines dominated finishing places in the Isle of Man TTs.

The overhead cam machines were expensive to prepare and, due to a change of policy at the factory, were phased out and replaced by an equally successful range of overhead valve machines. Starting as a humble 250cc MOV of 1933, this model was developed into the high-performance 350cc Viper and 500cc Venom and Thruxton variants. Again, these were very successful in clubman racing, at the TT, and at short circuits such as Thruxton in Hampshire: a Venom holds the world record for a 500cc machine by averaging over 100mph for a continuous 24 hours.

It is less well known, however, that Veloce also produced a wide range of two-stroke motorcycles exclusively, from 1913 to 1926, when an overhead cam (OHC) four-stroke was introduced. The two-stroke range then ran alongside the four-strokes until 1946, when the last model, the GTP, was discontinued.

The Second World War marked a change in Veloce policy. The directors had always held the view that there was a market for a motorcycle for 'every man' – an inexpensive machine of high quality and reliability that would satisfy the demand for mass transport – once hostilities had ceased, to satisfy the transport needs of a country recovering from six years of dislocation. They put aside the plans they had been working on to produce the world's first superbike, the Model O, and focused their attention on a small capacity commuter bike that would be attractive to people not accustomed to riding motorcycles.

The specification of this machine was very high, with quietness, comfort, lack of vibration, reliability and ease of maintenance considered important attributes to attract a new type of clientele. Thus it was that the LE range of twin-cylinder motorcycles was created, which drew on many of the designs and ideas developed when the two prototype twin-cylinder motorcycles, the Roarer and the Model O, were being created.

The LE caused a sensation when it was displayed at the 1948 Motorcycle Show in London, though the traditional motorcyclist was dismayed at the passing of the OHC Mk 2 KSS, and intended phasing out of the M series overhead valve (OHV) four-strokes so that the factory could concentrate on the LE. The LE can be likened to Marmite; either loved or hated. Such was the strength of feeling that when the Velocette Owners Club (VOC) was founded, it was targeted at owners of the single cylinder bikes, and LE owners formed their own club. This schism still exists today as a relic of the past, although, with the passage of time, the purity of

The Model O.

the LE design is beginning to be appreciated by many VOC members.

The purpose of this book is to show how the LE was developed from the ideas and designs generated when the twin-cylinder Roarer and Model O were being created. The same drawing boards and personnel were used in all cases, alongside the best brains that Veloce and, arguably, the entire motorcycle industry, had at that time. The Roarer and Model O were undoubtedly the superbikes of their era: hopefully, it will be seen that the LE should be considered the third member of the Velocette Twins family.

The book is presented in two parts. The first is an overview of the individuals involved with designing and developing the twin-cylinder bikes, and their contributions to other projects, the ideas they brought to Veloce Ltd, and their interactions and contributions to the company are discussed. Part two presents a technical examination of the Velocette twins, highlighting the ingenuity of the designs, and examining

the source and evolution of common design features. This part finishes with an overview of the preceding sections, summarising the main aspects, and conclusions that can be drawn from the book.

A postscript offers some information about post-war racing activities at Veloce, and the proposed development of a 4-cylinder 500cc racer. The company called in the receiver in 1971 following difficult trading conditions brought about by several projects that did not prove commercially viable.

Publisher's note
It is acknowledged that many images within this book are of poor quality: however, they are included because of their rarity and historical importance to the subject.

For those not familiar with maritime expressions, references to Port (left) and Starboard (right) are from the point of view of standing behind the machine.

Introduction:
In the beginning

The story of Velocette begins in a most unconventional manner, with the migration of Johannes Gütgemann in 1876 from Oberwinter on the Rhine, following the death of his father, and his aversion to military service. This was an unsettled time in European history, with Prussia making militaristic noises that persuaded many able-bodied young men to emigrate to Great Britain and elsewhere. The Gütgemann family was descended from Huguenots from the Alsace region, who relocated to Oberwinter, near Remagen in the 1570s. This area of Germany was a largely protestant region centred on Oberwinter.

The German centre of the Velocette Owners Club has recently taken an interest in the history

The house in Oberwinter on the Rhine: the birthplace of Johannes Gütgemann.

of the Gütgemann family, and, in 2019 , visited Oberwinter and identified the house, erected in 1776, where Johannes was born.

Johannes seems to have prospered in England for, in 1884, he married Elizabeth Orr and settled in Birmingham, where he took up a partnership with a Mr Barrett, who had inherited a pill-making company called Isaac Taylor and Co. At this point, Johannes began to use the name John Taylor in business (the name Gütgemann appeared on official documents of the time, and the rest of the family did not change their name to Goodman until 1917).

The pill company did very well, providing a surplus of funds that enabled John to buy out Mr Barrett. John was clearly very industrious, and, in 1891, is recorded as living at 56, Ingleby Street, Lady Wood, Birmingham, with his wife, Elizabeth Gütgemann (age 33; Birmingham-born), and their four children: six-year-old Percy; five-year-old Adele; Ethel, aged two years, and Eugene, five months.

Financial security provided by the pill-making company enabled John to diversify into the then-booming cycle business by opening a workshop adjacent to Great Hampton Street for the manufacture of cycle parts. This venture grew very well, and merged with a company owned by William Gue to form Taylor, Gue and Company, with the intention of manufacturing cycles under the trade name Hampton.

By 1901 the Gütgemanns were living at 3, Twyning Road, Edgbaston, Birmingham. John was classified as a cycle manufacturer and employer, and his son, Percy, was classified as a cycle (tool) manufacturer worker. The family continued to grow, with a fifth child Alfred (b 1892, d 1892) and a sixth Dora, born in 1898.

The success of Taylor, Gue and Company led, in 1904, to a joint venture with the maker of the Ormond motorcycle to produce the cycle parts for a new machine equipped with a Kelecom V twin engine. This seems to have been a false start as the venture soon folded, with Taylor Gue acquiring all the assets, enabling the company to manufacture a complete motorcycle. The first machine appeared in 1905, powered by a 402cc, inlet-over-side-exhaust engine with direct belt drive to the rear wheel. This machine was marketed under the name Veloce, but does not appear to have been a success.

Within a few months Taylor Gue Ltd ceased to trade and went into voluntary liquidation. Fortunately, John had seen potential in the developing cycle trade and, earlier in the year, with the backing of Edward Williams, a chain wheel manufacturer, had acquired premises off Spring Hill, Birmingham, and formed Veloce Ltd, manufacturing cycle parts and other sundry items, including roller skates. By this time the pill-making business had become a sideline, and was passed on to two family members.

John's sons, Percy and Eugene, were making their own way in life, not employed in the family business. Percy was apprenticed to a pattern maker, and ultimately went to India, where he became involved with the importation and sale of Wolseley cars. His brother, Eugene, served an apprenticeship in the tool room of the New Hudson Cycle Company in Birmingham.

In 1911, John Gütgemann turned 53 years of age, and is listed in the 1911 census as a cycle manufacturer and employer, living with his family in Edgbaston. Percy John Gütgemann was 26, and Eugene Frederick Gütgemann was 20, and they are listed as motor manufacturers and workers. In 1917, in response to anti-German sentiment, John Gütgemann and his family anglicised their name to Goodman by deed poll. The following extract is from the September 21st, 1917 issue of the *London Gazette* –

I, JOHN GOODMAN, heretofore called and known by the name of 'John Gütgemann,' of Number 112, Vivian Road, Harborne, in the city of Birmingham, Motor Cycle Manufacturer, hereby give public notice that, on the twenty-second day of August, one thousand, nine hundred and seventeen, I formally and absolutely renounced and abandoned the said surname of 'Gütgemann,' and declared that I had assumed and adopted and intended thenceforth upon all occasions whatsoever to use and subscribe the name of 'John Goodman' instead of 'John Gütgemann,' and so as to be at all times called and known and described by the name of 'John Goodman' exclusively. Dated this fourteenth day of September, 1917.
JOHN GOODMAN

The continued success of the cycle business, and the opening up of the motorcycle market, persuaded John to re-commence motorcycle production under the name Veloce in spite of the earlier setback. The family company board had John as Chairman until his death in 1929, when he was succeeded by his son, Percy, who continued in the post of Managing Director until his own death in 1953. Eugene was Works Director from when the company was founded, becoming Managing Director on Percy's death until his retirement in 1964. The post of MD then passed to Percy's son, Bertram, while Eugene's son, Peter, became Works Director. Ethel Goodman remained as Buyer and Company Secretary until her retirement in 1956. The only non-family member of the board in the inter-war years was Harold Willis, who became a director when his father purchased a large number of shares issued to capitalise the company, following the success of the OHC engine in the Isle of Man Junior TT of 1926.

The increase in demand for motorcycles following the 1926 TT win led to consolidation of production facilities as Veloce moved to its Hall Green factory on York road, previously occupied by Humphries and Dawes, maker of the OK-Supreme motorcycle. Veloce remained at this location until its liquidation in 1971.

Veloce and Velocette are the stuff of legend to motorcycle enthusiasts, their names firing the imagination of riders. The single cylinder machines produced in the 1920s and up to the beginning of the Second World War – which benefited from development that was led by a very successful factory racing programme – were, in many aspects, the forerunners of motorcycle design, and are consequently much sought-after today by discerning collectors.

Veloce was a family concern based upon the desire to produce a product of good value; not inexpensive, but one that reflected quality of design and workmanship, and was a pleasure to own. After all, to quote Henry Royce, "Quality remains long after the price is forgotten." Veloce strove to find a technically correct solution to any

The Veloce factory at York Road, Hall Green, Birmingham.

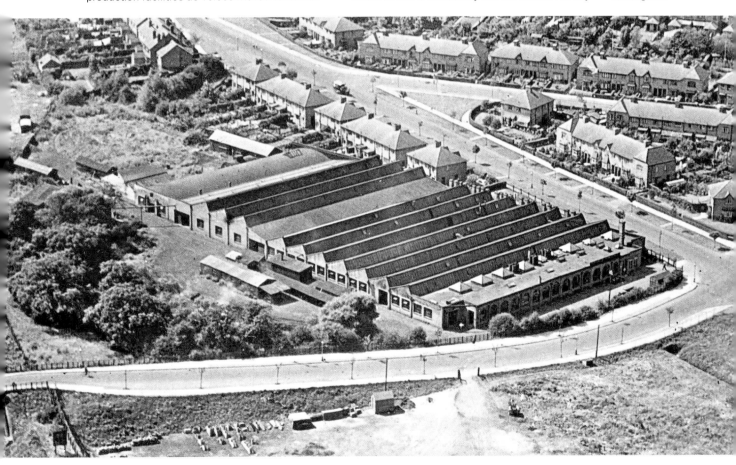

Mk 8 KTT of 1939.

problem, resulting in bikes of sometimes quirky character, but a policy that kept the company on the front line of motorcycle development.

Veloce enjoyed a very successful racing programme that resulted in three Junior TT wins in the twenties (1926, '28, '29), with valve tappet failure in 1927 forcing Bennett to retire and denying the company a clean sweep of four years.

The Veloce OHC engine was a revelation, quickly copied by other manufacturers, though its performance highlighted the shortcomings of the rest of the motorcycle. Veloce did not have another TT win until the late 1930s, after Stanley Woods was brought in to improve the frame design. There then followed a string of wins that were only interrupted by the Second World War, with victories in the 1937, 1938 and 1939 Junior TTs (Stanley Woods). When racing resumed, Velocettes were victorious in the 1947 (Bob Foster), 1948 (F L Frith), and 1949 (F L Frith) Junior TTs. Frith become World Champion in the latter year, winning every race of the series, with Bob Foster World Champion in 1950.

The Blue Riband of TT racing has always been the Senior event, dominated in the 1930s by main rival Norton. Private owners had entered KTTs in the Senior races and done reasonably well, but the factory decided to compete officially in the Senior TT. It produced two special 500 machines for Stanley Woods and Mellors to enter in the 1936 TT. Victory eluded Woods, however, and he finished second in 1936, followed by second places in '37 and '38, and a fourth in 1939.

The Goodman family recognised the value of a Senior TT victory, and concluded that a specialised machine was required to achieve this after watching the supercharged BMW machines, with plunger rear suspension and advanced telescopic forks. The shaft drive and oil tightness of the engine kept oil off the rear tyre, and the compact Zoller supercharger evened up the odds in relation to the British singles with their better riders.

Following a fundamental review of motorcycle design, preliminary design work on the new racing bike began in late 1938, incorporating the best parts of the BMW design with unique features. Construction began in early 1939, which resulted in a shakedown test at the

1939 TT. The Roarer, so-called by Willis because of its low frequency exhaust note, lapped the Mountain Circuit as a publicity venture, but was not in a satisfactory state of development to take part in the race itself. The Fédération Internationale de Motocyclisme (FIM) banned superchargers in 1946, thus relegating the forced induction Roarer to an interesting 'what might have been' had the Second World War not occurred.

Maintaining a works team was an expensive affair for a small family firm such as Veloce, but the publicity generated by racing victories – and resultant machine sales to the public – went some way toward offsetting this. The works racing machines were all 'Factory Specials':

essentially test beds designed to stretch overall design and components to the limit. The development work that this necessitated - perfecting and introducing many innovative ideas to the motorcycling world - resulted in Veloce producing the most technically advanced bikes. The positive stop foot gear change invented by Willis, and the first double overhead cam (DOHC) engine from Birmingham, designed by Charles Udall, are two notable examples.

Veloce was the first manufacturer to produce a 'Works Replica' machine for the general public, as close to the Factory Specials as it was practical to produce, and the success of the relatively large number of privateers competing successfully on KTTs in the TT is witness to this.

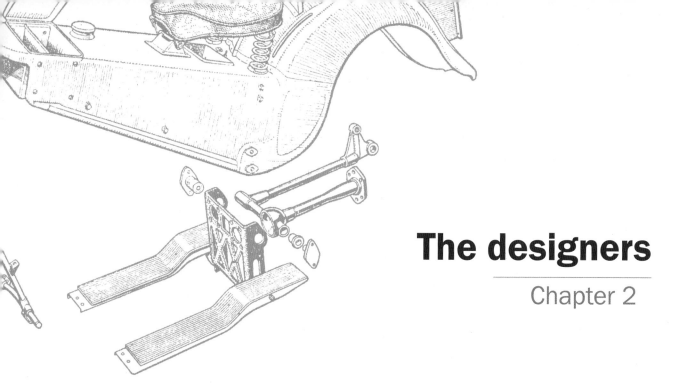

The designers

Chapter 2

Percy Goodman

It is evident that the formative years of Percy Goodman and his brother, Eugene, placed them in a very strong position to participate in the family business – from which they developed an interest in engineering – at the appropriate time. Percy was apprenticed to a pattern maker, but a chance meeting with an Indian Parsee, a customer for bicycles, saw him relocating to India, where he handled the importation of Wolseley cars.

Percy Goodman returned to Veloce unexpectedly in 1907 with the idea of manufacturing a motor car of his own design. With the encouragement of their father, he and Eugene set up a company called New Veloce Motors in the Spring Hill district of Birmingham. Percy focused on the design whilst Eugene concentrated on the production process. A prototype 20hp car was produced in 1908, but, despite the fact that the car was of sound design and construction, orders failed to materialise and the project was abandoned.

New Veloce diversified into general engineering, producing bicycle fittings and offering a plating service, but the business gradually ran down and was absorbed by Veloce Ltd in 1916. As the motorcycle market expanded, Percy decided to start work on a new motorcycle in the Fleet Street premises, and designed a machine that was remarkable for that era. The inlet over exhaust (IOE) two-speed 276cc

Veloce featured unit construction, and a two-speed transmission engaged by selective cone clutches operated by a rocking foot pedal. Oil was contained in a removable sump and was circulated by a gear pump driven off the end of the magneto shaft. Initially, the engine had an automatic inlet valve, but this was changed to a mechanically-operated IOE arrangement. The lack of response from potential customers made it apparent that such a design was far ahead of its time, and the design was shelved whilst a more conventional machine, not unlike the 500cc Triumph of that time, was produced. The 276cc machine was marketed under the trade name 'Veloce,' and the 500 was designated VMC, for Veloce Motor Company.

When the cycle car boom of 1912-1913 materialised, Veloce Ltd announced its intention to manufacture a V twin engine. Before this, in 1913, the company brought out a 206cc two-stroke, marketed under the trademark 'Velocette' (little Veloce). Veloce produced some very interesting two-stroke motorcycles for domestic use and for racing, with, initially, an automatic lubrication system under the control of the rider that gradually evolved to the throttle-controlled 'Posiforce' system in 1929 (sometime later, this system was 'reinvented' by a Japanese manufacturer).

Interest in a lightweight economy machine had been growing as motorcycling had become respectable, and John Goodman was perceptive enough to see that there would be a vast market, if only an 'Everyman' type of machine, requiring the minimum of maintenance, could be developed (this theme persisted throughout the entire history of the company as subsequent events will show). The Veloce two-stroke had at least two outstanding design features: an overhung crankshaft used in conjunction with a Desaxe cylinder and head, and a patent lubrication system in which oil was contained in a separate crankcase compartment and delivered to the various parts of the engine by exhaust pressure. Three models were available, the least expensive having direct belt drive, followed by a two-speed model with all-chain-drive. A ladies model – which featured a dropped 'open' frame – was also available. The Great War put paid to the V twin and the 276cc two-stroke, and the 500cc Triumph-like single as the company concentrated on war work, which included orders from Rolls-Royce. After the war, production focused on the two-strokes which were gradually developed and refined, with a three-speed model offered in 1921, fitted with a hub front brake designed by Percy Goodman; a year later a clutch was added, also designed by Percy.

With the 'Everyman' concept still in mind, a 'Light Two-Fifty' was announced in 1924, incorporating a revision to belt secondary drive, lightweight Brampton forks, and an exhaust pressurised lubrication system. It was in this year that the company looked to new horizons; no doubt taking note of the growing popularity of certain other manufacturers' products with overhead valve (OHV) four-stroke designs, and the complexity of two-stroke designs incorporating valves and other mechanical devices to boost power. An added incentive for the new design was the need for a high class production model that would uphold the company's reputation for performance and quality. Towards the end of 1923, mainly in his spare time in the bedroom of his son, Bertram, Percy Goodman had produced a set of drawings. The design had an OHC engine of 348cc with bevel-camshaft drive via a vertical shaft from the crankshaft. The requirement to use the then existing frames and gearboxes necessitated a very narrow crankcase that established the primary chain line inside that of the rear chain (this is a feature unique to Veloce that has been used ever since). This initial preliminary design featured a total loss oil system whereby oil was

supplied to the rocker box, and migrated to the big end and main bearings through the action of gravity and crankcase pressure.

The 1924 K engine designed by Percy Goodman with total loss oiling system.

The engine in this form was not a success, so it was reconfigured to include a gear-driven supply and scavenge oil pump located in the crankcase, providing positive oil feed to all the bearings and the rockers. This system was of the dry sump type, with an oil tank placed on the saddle tube feeding the pump through gravity flow. After initial teething troubles this engine was to be pre-eminent in the 350cc racing class for the next 25 years, winning the Junior TT in 1926, '28, '29, '38, and 1939, plus numerous continental GP wins and world championships in 1949 with Freddie Frith, and in 1950 with Bob Foster.

In the hands of Harold Willis this engine established several world records on the track at Brooklands and Montlhéry. Known as the Model K, it appeared in many guises: as the first factory replica to be offered to the public by any manufacturer (the KTT); as a sports version (the

Percy Goodman (on left) with Willis, Bennett and Hicks in the grounds of the Nursery Hotel, Onchan, after the 1928 Junior TT win.

KSS), and in touring specification as the KTS. A dirt track model was also produced, and known as the KDT. Several works specials of 500cc were produced to compete in the Senior TT, and a one-off 600cc version was produced for Stewart Waycott to compete on the International Six Days Trial (ISDT). Towards the end of its competitive life, several DOHC works specials of 250cc capacity were produced for riders such as Les Graham and Bill Lomas.

Percy Goodman is best known for his mechanical ingenuity, which he exercised in his hobby of watch repairing. Upon the death of John Goodman in 1929, Percy became Company Chairman, in which capacity he oversaw the growth of the company and ensured that the high standards of quality and integrity of design were maintained. Ill health dogged him during the Second World War, leading to his untimely death in 1953 – a difficult financial period in the company history – prompting the remaining family members to decide to close the Race Shop, thus curtailing racing activities and bringing to a premature end the development of a four-cylinder 500cc racing motorcycle that Percy had been working on with his son, Bertram.

Eugene Goodman

It might appear from previous paragraphs that Percy's younger brother, Eugene, was almost a shadowy figure in the background at Veloce Ltd, working on the day-to-day production processes in the factory. In reality, Eugene had served an apprenticeship in the tool room of the New Hudson Works in Birmingham, and was a keen motorcyclist who took an active interest in the development of the Veloce motorcycles.

In the 1930s sales had fallen to half or even a third of the level achieved in the 1920s. Concerned at the small amount of business the company was doing, Eugene felt that a less expensive machine with the build quality of a Velocette – which could be built more economically than the OHC models – would find a ready market.

The first prototype comprised a frame and cycle parts of the production GTP two-stroke machine, carrying a 350cc sidevalve engine designed by Phil Irving. This design was intended to use up stocks of obsolete parts from the early K engine, but poor performance and lack of mechanical quietness from this under-developed

Final evolution of Percy Goodman's K: the Works Special DOHC of 1954, designed by Bertram Goodman.

engine led to Eugene designing a replacement high camshaft pushrod 250cc OHV machine of 68mm bore and stroke. The valve layout closely followed that of the Riley car engine well known for its performance in the hands of Freddy Dixon. A prototype machine was produced that used a new frame design and a new four-speed gearbox that was a lightweight version of the gearboxes found on the KSS and KTS models.

This was, perhaps, the first incarnation of the 'everyman machine,' which was known as the MOV. The M followed the usual Veloce model type designation, and it's assumed that OV stood for 'Overhead Valve.' The MOV was well received by the buying public, to the extent that a larger capacity 350cc single was produced by the expedient of lengthening the stroke to 96mm. It was thus possible to use the same piston, valves and cylinder head casting as the smaller engine, so very few parts were not interchangeable between the two models. The new model was clearly of M type and became known as the MAC; quite why the letters AC were appended is open to conjecture, but it has been suggested that they stand for 'Additional Capacity.' These models were the forerunners of the famous M series of pushrod singles, including the 350cc Viper, the 500cc MSS, Venom, Scrambler, Endurance, and the Thruxton: all recognised by their characteristic

'Map of Africa' timing cover. The MAC proved the most profitable bike in the company's history.

As a production engineer Eugene was clearly concerned about production costs, and realised that the orthodox form of motorcycle, with its separate engine and gearbox and a tubular frame built up of a multiplicity of machined lugs, was a very expensive process. He must have discussed his ideas on mass production with Phil Irving, who was then at Veloce as development work began on a prototype frame incorporating a stressed skin rear section matched to the front section and steering head of a conventional frame. Eugene must have had sufficient confidence in the pressed steel frame to instruct Irving to proceed with the design of the roadgoing version of the

Eugene Goodman on an IoE Veloce, taking part in the Coventry MCC's Open One Day Trial, May 22, 1913.

supercharged twin racer, and purchased a Lake Erie hydraulic press to produce the pressings. The company enamelling and plating plants had also been reorganised to a conveyor type of operation that greatly increased capacity. Unfortunately, circumstances over which the company had no control ended civilian motorcycle production when World War 2 was declared in 1939.

During the war much thought was given to the evolution of a new design to meet expected demand, post-hostilities. Discussion with Phil Irving undoubtedly occurred, and, when Phil was bedridden due to a shrapnel injury sustained in an air raid on Birmingham in 1941, Eugene arranged for a drawing board to be taken to Phil's house. Here, Phil commenced work on layout drawings of a new lightweight motorcycle embodying some of the specifications discussed earlier. Central to the design was the ability to produce large numbers economically to meet expected demand for personal transport following cessation of hostilities.

Sometime later, after Irving had left Veloce to work at Associated Motor Cycles (AMC), Charles Udall underwent an operation for appendicitis, and, whilst convalescing at home, he undertook to carry on with the design; accordingly provided with a drawing board and Irving's drawings. In due course Udall produced a much more sophisticated design that embodied many of the ideas talked of, but which differed from Irving's layout in several respects.

When Udall's drawings were sent to a parts supplier for evaluation it was noticed that the drawings were without a name. In haste, when asked for one, the person concerned mentioned that this was a 'Little Engine,' which became abbreviated to LE and the name stuck from then on.

Veloce had very high expectations for the LE, the culmination of Eugene Goodman's dream, the 'everyman machine,' and the plan was for Veloce to eventually cease making all other models to concentrate on just the new design. An output of 300 machines per week was planned, which required a complete redesign of the factory, with the power and transmission units being assembled on a track. Reorganising the factory and reducing output of the singles led to financial strain on the already depleted company assets.

Many consider that the LE forced Veloce into liquidation in the early 1970s. A great deal of the profit accumulated fulfilling War Ministry contracts was used in producing tooling for the new design. It proved not possible to achieve the anticipated output of 300 machines a week; the best was around 165. This lack of orders forced the company to reinstate production of the singles and focus on developing more attractive variations of the LE.

The LE was not looked upon favourably by the buying public, but did find a niche market with several police forces, which favoured the quiet running and reliability that the design offered. Inevitably, large discounts for bulk orders for machines and spares were demanded, which meant that profit margin on these sales was very small.

MOV 250cc, designed by Eugene Goodman, which led to the 350cc MAC.

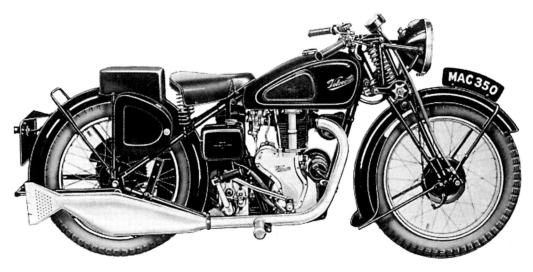

MAC 350cc.

Harold Willis

Harold Willis was the senior of the three designers who had a hand in the Velocette Twins, and unusual in that he was the only company director who was not a member of the Goodman family. Born in Kings Norton, Worcestershire, in 1900 to Eliza and Sidney C Willis, he was one of four children. Little is known of his formative years, although he served in the Royal Navy in the First World War, and unfortunately was torpedoed at Jutland, resulting in him being immersed in sea water for several hours before he was rescued. The subsequent damage to his respiratory system lasted for the rest of his life, and indirectly led to his untimely death in 1939.

As a young man Willis was a keen motorcyclist, competing regularly in many events, including the TT. As Table 2.1 (page 22) shows, from 1924 to 1932 he competed on a variety of machines before settling on Velocette.

Following the 1926 TT victory, Velocette motorcycles were in such demand that it was necessary to find larger premises, and the site chosen was the Hall Green works formerly the home of Humphries and Dawes, maker of the OK Supreme. To finance the move Veloce approached its bank manager, but when a loan was refused a shares issue was offered to the public. This was mostly bought by Harold's father, a prominent businessman in Birmingham. Mr Willis senior was founder of the Midlands Cattle Products company, and a large cattle dealer supplying livestock to the War Office. He was a partner of Willis Bros, a large business that occupied significant premises in Birmingham Cattle Market, sat on various government committees dealing with meat control in the First World War, and was also a member of the Commission on Abattoir Design. By the time of his death he was chairman of four companies dealing with meat by-products.

The purchase of the shares by his father bought Harold a seat on the Board, where he took over the responsibilities of Race Shop Manager, Tester, Overseer of the Drawing Office, General Mr Fixit and Technical Director. Harold had an immediate impact on Veloce fortunes by being a record-breaker at Brooklands, where he set several records. He also had a string of long distance records at Montlhéry in 1928, including the first to achieve over 100 miles in the hour (100.3mph). Willis was very much of the opinion that extending the performance of his special machines beyond the normal envelope, in the form of racing and record-breaking, provided information that could be used to improve the standard product.

The record-breaking engine featured several changes that were later adopted for the production engines. In the special engine the compression ratio was raised to 10.5:1, which required a reduction in the radius of the hemispherical cylinder head, which also involved a reduction in the exhaust valve diameter, and the machining of a cutaway in the piston crown to provide clearance for the valve (similar modifications were made by Vic Willoughby to his 1939 KTT to improve performance).

The exhaust valve was of KE965 steel – tulip-shaped with a heavy stem – whilst the inlet valve featured a flat head with a light stem. The valves were well supported by cast iron valve guides projecting into the polished ports. A standard No 24 cam was used that provided valve timing of Exhaust Valve Opening (EVO) 60 degrees Before Top Dead Centre (BTDC), exhaust Valve Closing (EVC) 45 degrees After Top Dead Centre (ATDC), Inlet Valve Opening (IVO) 38 degrees Before Top Dead Centre (BTDC), Inlet Valve Closing (IVC) 58 degrees After Bottom Bead

Partially dismantled engine used for the 24-hour record in 1928.

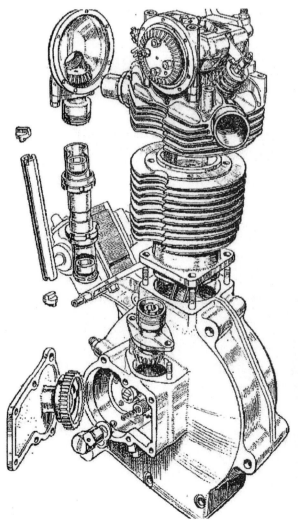

Centre (ABDC). This produced an 83 degree valve overlap: quite mild by modern standards but resulting in a very tractable motor.

The slipper-type piston with two piston rings was used, weighing 10oz (280gm). The hollow fully floating gudgeon pin of $^{13}/_{16}$in (20.8mm) diameter was retained by spring circlips at each end. The connecting rod big end – which contained uncaged rollers – was slightly wider and of larger diameter than normal (but it did became the standard for the production engines). To retain crank stiffness at the prolonged high speeds of record-breaking, a special set of crankcases was produced with wall thickness of $^{5}/_{8}$in (15.875mm). This feature led to stiffening webs being added to the KTT crankcases, providing enhanced stiffness with a small weight penalty.

The remainder of the high performance engine was standard in design and material. The frame was the standard item used by Willis in the TT, with the usual cup and cone steering head and the usual cylinder head steady from the front down tubes. The saddle was, however, set further back than usual to accommodate a $4^{1}/_{2}$ gallon (20.43 litre) fuel tank.

For record-breaking attempts the front brake was not fitted, while the seat location allowed the rear brake pedal to be sited on the brake backplate. The wheels of 27 x 2.75 size were fully balanced and fitted with Dunlop racing tyres. Webb side strutted forks provided the steering, and Coventry Ultimate chains were fitted, as was a square ML magneto and an Amal TT carburettor.

Roaring Anna, so-called by Willis, went on to break the five kilometre (flying start) record at 106.92mph (172km/hr), and the ten miles (standing start) at 104mph (167.36km/hr). The machine is still in existence in the Rhodes Collection. It appeared in track form with the Venom 24-hour record-breaker at Montlhéry in 2011 to celebrate the 50th anniversary of Velocette taking the record of averaging over 100 miles per hour for 24 hours.

Harold Willis was a successful TT rider in his own right as well as a very practical and inventive engineer. He was second in the Junior TTs of 1927 and 1928, and also won the 1927 Hutchinson 100 at Brooklands at an average speed of 86mph (138.4km/hr). As an experienced rider, Willis was aware of the

Roaring Anna in track form following the first successful 100 miles in the hour at Montlhéry, 1928.

At Brooklands on May 4, 1934, Les Archer smashed the 100mph record with an average speed of 79.52mph. (Courtesy Fox Photos)

Table 2.1   IOM TT race results of H J Willis

Year	Machine	Position	Time hr.min.sec	Average speed mph (km/hr)
1932 Junior	Velocette	DNF		
1931 Junior	Velocette	11	3.50.30	68.76 (110.65)
1930 Junior	Velocette	DNF		
1929 Junior	Velocette	DNF		
1928 Junior	Velocette	2	3.56.00	67.16 (108.07)
1927 Junior	Velocette	2	4.06.39	63.42 (102.05)
1926 Senior	Triumph	12	4.19.35	60.39 (97.18)
1925 Junior	Montgomery	DNF		
1925 Senior	Montgomery	9	3.43.48	60.7 (97.68)
1924 Junior	Montgomery	5	4.17.19	52.8 (84.96)

time lost when changing gear with the then conventional hand-operated control. This inspired him to develop the now universally adopted foot change positive stop mechanism. There had been prior attempts at foot control of the gearchange based on arranging the change lever to be close to the foot, but the Willis design incorporated a fixed ratcheted positive stop drive that returned the gear lever to a central position. Originally designed as an aftermarket fitting to existing gearboxes, the positive stop mechanism was attached to the outside of the gearbox. With the introduction of a four-speed box, the positive stop mechanism was contained inside this, and the earlier design was sold to the Scott Company. A similar design was used by Moto Guzzi until the 1960s.

Veloce was among the first manufacturers to anticipate the rush to supercharging, in spite of the difficulty of merging a steady flow device (compressor) to an unsteady, pulsating flow reciprocating engine. The ever-inventive Phil Irving initiated experimentation with supercharging in 1931 by applying a vacuum

The Willis-designed positive stop gearchange mechanism.

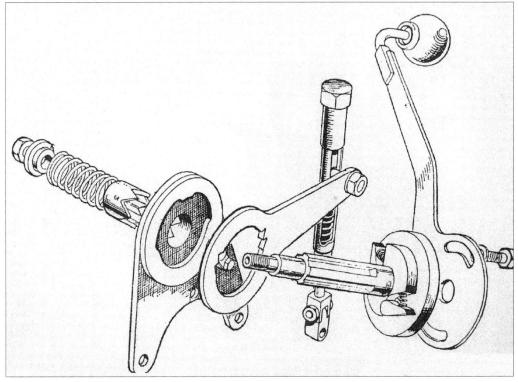

Willis and Bennett: 2nd and 1st in the 1928 Junior TT.

cleaner blower to a KTT engine (KTT 240) in the Veloce engine test shop. This boosted output from 22bhp to 30bhp, much to the delight of all concerned. The engine was passed to Willis, who began further experimenting with forced induction using a Foxwell supercharger with a six-vane eccentric rotor. It is said he favoured this make because of the way the vanes were supported in end plates.

The initial arrangement, with the supercharger placed ahead of the crankcase, had the supercharger blowing through the carburettor, which required the fuel tank and the float chamber to be pressurised in order for petrol to flow to the carburettor, and the required depression to be maintained over the fuel jets. In 1932, the plumbing was rearranged to a much simpler form with the blower positioned between the carburettor and the cylinder, separated by a plenum chamber (the 'official receiver' in Willis-speak) that damped out pulsation induced by the engine. A flame trap and a second

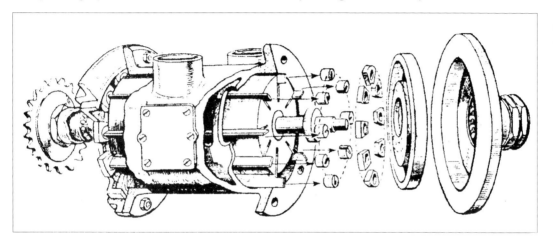

Foxwell supercharger as used on Whiffing Clara.

carburettor body were placed between the receiver and cylinder head to act as a throttle control, and reduce lag to throttle response. The result of these changes was a machine of startling performance, combining docility with unprecedented acceleration. Whiffling Clara, as the bike became known because of the noises made when evacuating the plenum chamber, was entered in both Junior and Senior TTs, but retired in the Junior with a broken rocker and with a loose carburettor jet in the Senior. Veloce, a tiny firm to take on such an ambitious programme, then put supercharging onto the back burner until 1938/39, when, with enormous pride and patriotism, it designed the Roarer to take on the might of the BMW twins and the Gilera fours.

It is doubtful Willis thought that supercharging would produce a world-beater but, as a development engineer, he recognised the benefits to be had by testing KTT components to the utmost degree. The engine – initially assembled with standard components – stood up to the increased stresses very well, and there was no trouble with melted pistons, as was often the case with supercharging, although the sparkplugs were punished very badly. To overcome this the factory developed a cylinder head produced in aluminium-bronze that improved cooling, which was fitted to the Mk 4 KTT.

Clara is, fortunately, still with us in the Rhodes Collection, having recently received a makeover. Harold Willis was undoubtably an excellent development engineer, but Phil Irving considered him too conservative a rider to be a full-blown racer, as Willis' preference was for equipment and riding style more suited to record-breaking. Willis refused to use a twist grip throttle, preferring instead a short stubby lever as used by the Brooklands fraternity, which could be set when flat out and thereafter left alone whilst the rider focussed on the steering. Charles Udall was critical of Willis' analytical ability, which could explain why Clara was not developed, and why Willis was taken in by the Aspin rotary valve cylinder head.

The Aspin head consisted essentially of a rotating conical combustion chamber that, as it rotates at half crankshaft speed, sweeps across an inlet port; a sparkplug and an exhaust port to facilitate the normal induction, ignition expansion and exhaust cycle. It is a very attractive proposition inasmuch as it does away with the inlet and exhaust valves and valve springs that were a persistent source of trouble in the 1930s, and eliminated torque fluctuations on the valve drive which sometimes caused the timing gears to fail. The inventor, Frank Aspin, claimed that a 250cc engine fitted with his rotary valve cylinder

Willis' supercharged K on Whiffing Clara with positive stop foot gearchange mechanism.

head had produced 24hp at 12,000rpm on test: double the power output of a normal engine and at a speed that would usually destroy roller bearing big ends. The KTT was safe to 8000rpm with a caged roller, and it is not clear how fitting the Aspin head might extend the life of the big end bearing if these revs were exceeded.

The normally sceptical Willis was convinced by Aspin, however, and an agreement was signed whereby Veloce would develop an Aspin head for the 1937 TT, with the condition that the agreement be confidential. Had the engine been a success Veloce would have had exclusive rights to the technology for one year. Unknown to Willis, however, Aspin then went to BSA and signed a similar agreement, using the Veloce agreement as an incentive. Unfortunately, in reality, the head did not live up to expectations and was a major distraction that delayed development of the Mk 6 KTT and the factory racers of 1937.

With hindsight it is clear that some basic calculations would have shown the falsehood of the claims made by Aspin with respect to power output and efficiency ...

It is interesting that Phil Irving, who was working at Veloce at the time, clearly had reservations, but his views were initially ignored. Irving has stated that Willis was not skilled in draughtsmanship, and nor could he sketch, so relied heavily on Charles Udall to bring his ideas to fruition.

On June 11, 1939, and on the eve of Stanley Woods winning the Junior IOM TT on a Velocette, tragically, Harold Willis died following a medical procedure to relieve the sinus problems he had suffered for over 20 years. He is buried in the graveyard of St Mary's Church in Llanfair, Wales, alongside his mother, Eliza (1864-1961), and his uncle, Major Justin C Willis, who died in August 1918 from wounds suffered in action whilst serving in France in the Great War.

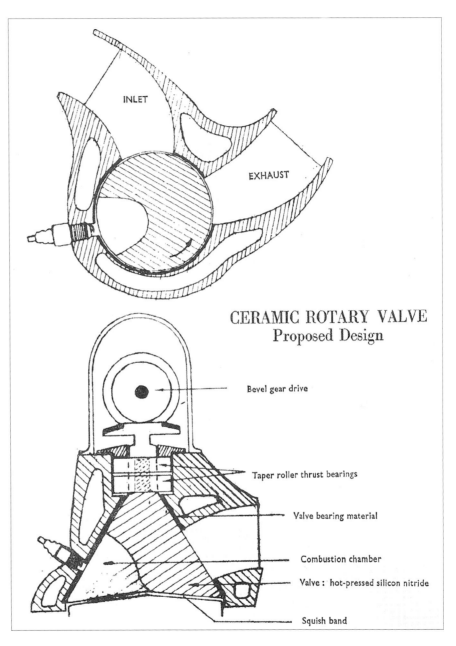

INLET

EXHAUST

CERAMIC ROTARY VALVE
Proposed Design

Bevel gear drive

Taper roller thrust bearings

Valve bearing material

Combustion chamber

Valve : hot-pressed silicon nitride

Squish band

Aspin rotary valve.

Charles Udall

Charles Udall was born in Birmingham in 1911 to a well-to-do family. His father, who was the accountant for British Insulated Callander's Cables (BICC), secured Charles his first employment with this company, although this did not work out as expected and Charles soon left to join a company making electrical meters. Eventually, his father arranged, through business contacts, for Charles to meet and be interviewed by John Goodman, and Charles started work at Veloce in the repair shop in 1927, beginning a long association with Velocette.

After a year there, Charles heard of a vacancy in the drawing office, and, following an opportune conversation with Percy Goodman, was offered the post. One of his first jobs as a junior draftsman was production of detail design drawings of the MOV that had been designed by Eugene Goodman. This job was completed during the 1932 TT practice and race period when the drawing office was quiet, with most of the other occupants away at the Isle of Man.

Charles Udall was a very competent engineer and draughtsman with a keen analytical mind, and was able to approach problems from first principles; quite a contrast to Willis. He joined the racing shop in 1933 where his skills developed, although he seems to have kept his talents hidden. This may have been through shyness, management policy, or his relationship with Willis, which seems to have stifled his individuality. Udall had to persuade the Board to agree to develop the 1936 DOHC engine – the first DOHC engine to come out of Birmingham.

Apart from a short period at AMC towards the end of his career, Charles spent the remainder of his working life at Veloce.

Harold Willis quickly dropped this DOHC

Left below: 1936 double overhead cam cylinder head designed by Charles Udall. (Courtesy The Motor Cycle)

Right: Double overhead cam engine at Fellside.

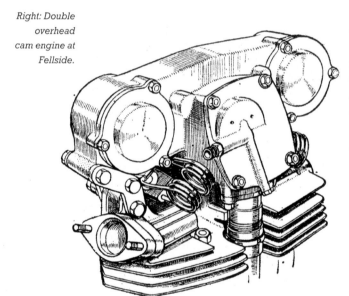

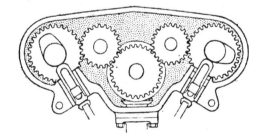

motor when the bike ridden by Stanley Woods stopped on the first lap of the TT due to failure of an Oldham coupling in the cam drive: a hitherto unheard of event. No more was seen of this DOHC design on the IOM, but examples did perform well on the continental circus, and have subsequently performed well in Australia to where they were banished. Further developments by Udall led to the waisting of the cam drive shaft, to introduce torsional flexibility into the drive and reduce shock loading of the coupling. In this form, the motor could be safely taken to 8400rpm when the SOHC motor was limited to 7000rpm. Willis seems to have lost interest in the DOHC as he was engaged with the Aspin rotary valve project, KTT development, and ideas concerning the Roarer. Stanley Woods considered dropping the DOHC to have been a major mistake as his bike was so fast that he was expected to win the 1936 TT at a canter. The other company directors were all disappointed that Willis

dropped the DOHC, but as he was in charge of the racing programme, felt they had to back his decision.

Following the death of Willis in 1939, Udall took on his duties in developing the Roarer and leading the Drawing Office; eventually becoming Technical Director at Veloce.

Towards the end, when the company was in dire financial straits, Veloce had to seek capital from external financiers. Help was forthcoming, but conditional upon the company directors offering their houses as collateral. The Goodmans asked Charles to do the same with his property, to which he replied, understandably, that he could not put his family in such a situation. After this the relationship between him and the family directors deteriorated to the extent that Udall departed to work for AMC, where he received double his Veloce salary!

Charles was happy at AMC because he felt valued; people listened to him and made

1936 DOHC engine in sprung frame with Stanley Woods at the Isle of Man TT.

Charles Udall (right) with Stanley Woods and the Roarer.

him feel welcome. He solved several technical problems that had been bearing down on the Matchless and AJS twins, and is remembered for designing the P10, a 800/850 OHC twin produced in prototype form only as the directors of AMC abandoned the project. The P10 is now in the National Motorcycle Museum in Birmingham.

In 1969 AMC called in the receivers, and, at the age of 58, Charles Udall found himself unemployed, though felt he still had a lot to give the industry. He returned to Veloce for 18 months until the company went into voluntary receivership in 1971. In an interview recorded for the Velocette Owners Club magazine of February 2003 (No 329), Charles looked back at his time at Veloce with mixed feelings. As he said "If I had been more outspoken, things might have been different ..."

Phil Irving

Few automotive engineers can claim to have designed both a record-breaking motorcycle engine and a Formula 1 championship-winning car engine. Phil Irving can, however, be included in that number, being responsible for the Vincent V Twin and the Repco Engine that won two F1 championships in a Brabham

Phil Irving was born in Australia, where he received a technical education. He began work in 1922 for the Australian engineer Anthony Michell at the firm of Crankless Engines Ltd. Between 1926 and 1931 Irving jointly owned and operated a motorcycle workshop in the regional town of Ballarat, Australia, with partner Ken Granter. As the economic climate worsened in 1929, business at the shop slumped, forcing it to close. In 1931, Irving left Australia and travelled to Britain as pillion passenger to the adventurer John Gill on his round-the-world motorcycle and sidecar journey, an epic trip that was sponsored by the HRD-Vincent Company. On arrival in Britain, the pair travelled to Stevenage where Philip Vincent and Phil Irving commenced a lifelong friendship. Irving had two stints working for Vincent at Stevenage: the first in the early thirties until 1937, and then again from 1943 as Chief Engineer.

From 1937 to 1942 Irving worked for Velocette at its Hall Green factory in Birmingham, where he designed and patented a number of ideas, including the famed rear suspension adjustment used on the post-war spring-frame Velocettes, and also the LE Velocette. Irving also designed and built the prototype Model 'O' Velocette that employed the geared crankshafts used on the Roarer. A significant design undertaken by Irving whilst at Veloce was for a four-stroke version of the 'everyman motorcycle.' This consisted of a single-cylinder sidevalve engine of 74 x 81mm bore and stroke, making 348cc displacement. The machine was designed to weigh less than 224lb, as it would then qualify for a reduced road tax levy. Veloce, at that time, had on hand a surplus of cast iron flywheels, lightweight conrods and low crown pistons from the vintage K models, as these components had been superseded by improved designs (including steel flywheels for the camshaft models). Presumably, had the usual Veloce machine designation been followed, this new model would have become the MSV, had it gone into production.

Initially, the engine was placed in a GTP frame whilst Irving worked on a new design of frame and cycle parts. The performance of the sidevalve engine was disappointing, which led Eugene Goodman to design the MOV, and the new frame and cycle parts were used for this model. The square bore and stroke of the MOV (68 x 68) may well have been determined by the fact that Harold Willis had had some experience with a KTT of 68mm bore and a stroke of 96mm that he called 'the bicycle pump motor.' Availability of factory tooling could have influenced the decision to use the same measurements for the MAC. The 96mm stroke was also used on the works 500cc racers, and on the iron MSS with an 81mm bore.

Phil Irving was a very competent

Prototype MSV engine designed by Phil Irving; now owned by the Seymour family.

motorcyclist, especially favouring to drive a sidecar outfit. His great experience in this mode of transport made him the ideal person to design a sidecar for Bristol dealer Stuart Waycott to use in the 1937 International Six Days Trial (ISDT). The outfit was powered by a one-off 600cc OHC engine, the largest made by Veloce. Irving based his designs on an Australian Goulding sidecar, which he strengthened and modified to take the greater stresses experienced when completing the ISDT course. These improvements included a braked and sprung wheel, and a four-point mounting to the bike frame. Adjustable clamps were fitted to the $^{1}/_{4}$ elliptic leaf springs to provide the sidecar body with anti-roll damping. A single leg stand was provided for sidecar

Frame and cycle parts designed by Phil Irving; later used for the MOV.

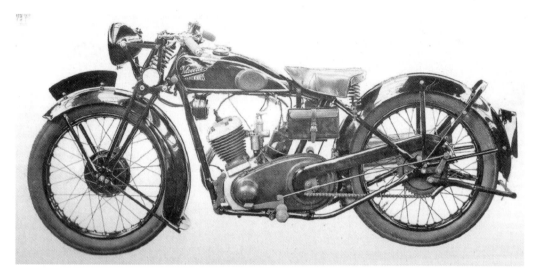

wheel changes. The body – which carried a spare wheel, compressed air bottles and tools – could be swung up vertically to allow access to the driveside of the machine. A special plug spanner was made with a catch inside it to hold the plugs so that changing could be done with the rider or passenger sitting in the 'chair' or on the machine. A varied selection of gearbox sprockets was carried, providing suitable ratios for either trials or roadwork.

Stuart Waycott had no trouble winning the 1937 and 1938 ISDT, and later confirmed he had never enjoyed the comfort and reliability of a competition sidecar outfit more. The approaching Second World War prevented its use in 1939.

In 1942 Irving moved to London and worked with Joe Craig at Associated Motor Cycles Ltd (AMC) at Plumstead. In July 1943, Phillip Vincent wrote to Irving, inviting him to return to the Vincent HRD company at Stevenage to develop the opposed piston two-stroke engine that was intended to be fitted to an eleven-man airborne lifeboat then under development. Irving remained at Stevenage until 1949, when he returned home to Australia.

During the 1930s and '40s, Phil Irving wrote a technical column in *Motor Cycling* magazine under the pseudonym 'Slide Rule.' Some of his articles were later reprinted in book form as *Motorcycle Technicalities*. Amongst the other books he authored are *Tuning for Speed, Motorcycle Engineering,* and the well-read *Phil Irving – An Autobiography.*

At the 1960 Isle of Man TT Races, Dr Josef Ehrlich, owner of Ehrlich Motor Cycles (EMC), commissioned Irving to 'reverse-engineer' a 125cc racing engine supplied by Ehrlich, and to produce the working drawings of a water-cooled variant that became the 1961 EMC 125cc water-cooled single cylinder racing engine. This was followed, in 1963, by an approach by Formula 1 team owner and driver Jack Brabham for Irving to design a simple, lightweight and powerful 3-litre V8 engine for the 1966 racing season. This engine was built around the 3.5-litre Oldsmobile V8 cylinder block design, and became known as the RB620. It incorporated some off-the-shelf technology such as Vincent valve inspection caps and BSA 500cc Gold Star cam profiles. Jack Brabham won the 1966 Formula 1 Driver's Championship and the Manufacturers' Championship using this engine.

In 1949 Irving became Vice President of the Vincent HRD Owners Club, continuing in this role until the death of Phil Vincent in 1979 when he was elected to the vacant post of Club President (an honorary title), holding the presidency until his death on 14 January, 1992. Phil Irving was awarded an MBE (Member of the British Empire) in the Queen's 1976 New Year Honours list for his "services to automotive engineering." In later life, Irving lived permanently in Australia, basing himself at Warrandyte on the outskirts of Melbourne, where he had a small workshop. He never ceased his practical involvement with engines and especially with Vincent motorcycles. Just a few weeks before his death, aged 89, he was still working on Harley-Davidson motorcycles at Midwest Harley in Ballarat, Australia. Its owner, Ken James, said: "You can't stop Phil; he just needs to be around engines and make them sing."

Irving was a different kettle of fish to Udall, being more independently-minded and unlikely to be as subservient. He was an accomplished automotive engineer with an emphasis on designing for production. His motorcycle engine designs were ingenious, and incorporated many features then found only on car engines.

Stanley Woods

It is not the intention here to imply that Stanley Woods was responsible for any of the design work on the Roarer and Model O, but it is irrefutable that he had an influence on the racing fortunes of Veloce Ltd, and made a significant contribution to improving the works specials by suggesting changes that would have trickled down to the Twins. Stanley Woods was brought into the Veloce racing team at the request of Percy Goodman, who recognised that Veloce needed to retain a rider of Stanley's ability in order to regain its rightful place in motorcycle racing.

Veloce's fortunes had been waning following a successful period from 1926 to 1929 when it won three Junior TTs (1926, 1928, 1929), and Willis was second in 1927 when failure of a new design of tappet adjustment put the rest of the works team out of the race.

It was at the 1935 TT that Percy Goodman approached Stanley with an offer to take out one of the works Velocettes for a practice lap, upon completion of which Stanley offered the opinion that the motor was very good but the handling was bad, and the gear ratios were all wrong.

It must be remembered that Stanley Woods was, at this time, a professional freelance rider interested only in winning, in which capacity he had ridden several different makes of motorcycle, including Cotton, Harley-Davidson, DKW, Norton, and Moto Guzzi, winning both the Lightweight and Senior TTs on a Moto Guzzi in 1935. Soon after the TT, Stanley received a letter from Percy Goodman asking for his assistance. The text of this letter follows.

Stanley Woods Esq
Mount Merrion Park
Black Rock
Co Dublin

Dear Sir
After this year's experience in the TT I feel that we shall not do any good until we secure the services of a rider such as yourself. I should therefore like to discuss with you (as soon as you are in a position to do so) arrangements for next year.

We desire to discuss this at the earliest possible moment so that we can take immediate steps to develop a machine suitable for next year.

We consider it necessary to have the assistance of a rider like yourself in order to develop the machine so that it will handle properly on the course.

As soon as you have time I should be glad if you would get into touch with me personally.
Yours sincerely,

The comments made by Stanley about the performance of the works Velocettes begs the question how had they got into this state? It is a relatively straightforward exercise to use a Tractive Effort Velocity Graph to determine a correct set of gearbox ratios for a particular application, and the riders should have been aware of the handling problems. Is this another example of poor communication from the boardroom?

At this time – the 1930s – Moto Guzzis were arguably the most technically advanced motorcycles available to the public. Company owners and designers Carlo Guzzi and Giorgio Parodi served in the Italian Air Force in the First World War, where they developed their own ideas about motorcycle design. Their unit construction single cylinder engine was laid horizontally in the frame, with the cylinder head close behind the front wheel. This approach is quite different to the ideas of Harold Willis, who developed the large-finned Huntly and Palmer head of high thermal conductivity aluminum in order to place the cooling fins outside the boundary layer of the front wheel (arguably a flawed idea as a rotating wheel acts as a pump that could circulate air around an engine). Working from first principles of aircraft design, Carlo Guzzi realised that the centre of mass of a projectile should be placed ahead of the centre of pressure in order to achieve directional stability (just as in ship design the centre of buoyancy has to be below the centre of mass). The Guzzi layout supported this proposition. Willis, on the other hand, considered that the engine should be moved back in the frame to apply more weight to the back wheel to keep it in contact with the road.

The 1935 Senior TT-winning Guzzi had cantilever rear suspension with the springs contained in boxes that ran under the engine. The suspension pivot was on the frame fastened to the back of the engine-gearbox unit. Friction dampers of Andre-type were attached to the top subframe and the suspension arm, and were adjustable by using a lever mounted on the fuel tank on Woods' TT bike, but this feature was discontinued on production bikes. The frame was cleverly designed to be split above the suspension pivots and at the front engine mount, enabling the front suspension and wheel, the top part of the frame (including the fuel and oil tanks), and the rear subframe to be removed, leaving behind the engine-gearbox unit, rear suspension and wheel. Another example of an integrated drive unit.

Carlo Guzzi was also very interested in analysing the forces acting on the components of a motorcycle in order to ensure that they were fit for purpose. This is evident in a picture of the 1935 TT-winning Guzzi machine, which

clearly shows a front brake torque arm running from the top of the girder fork blade to the brake backplate: a feature adopted on the works 500cc Velocette in 1937, and subsequently used on all works specials and production racing bikes.

Upon joining Veloce in the autumn of 1935, Stanley Woods spent some time at Hall Green developing a new frame for the works specials, which were tested on the island with lead weights placed at different positions to establish satisfactory weight distribution and new frame geometry. The new frames were then taken to Switzerland by Ernie Thomas in May 1936 for further testing with the lead weights. The final iteration was tested by means of a high speed seven-lap run at the Isle of Man. Subsequently, a new swing arm frame was designed, incorporating a new steering head lug which steepened the front down tube, bringing it closer to the front wheel, and thus enabling the engine to be placed further forward in the frame. The new design was used in the 1936 TT, and the improved designs were then produced for production in 1937. Several other important changes to the rear brake and swing arm pivot spindle were applied at the same time.

Stanley Woods was one of the most successful motorcycle racers of his time. He received a generous retainer from Veloce, complemented by bonus payments from component and oil manufacturers. In 1938 he received an annual retainer of £400.00 from Veloce, which also agreed to pay his expenses – amounting to £23.14.6. – for the TT. In addition, Woods received the bonuses shown in the following table:

Table 2.2   Stanley Woods' TT expenses

Awarding body	Bonus paid £
ACU for appearance money for riding in the TT	150.00
Ferodo Ltd for using its brake material	50.00
KLG Sparking Plugs Ltd	50.00
Dunlop Rubber Co Ltd for using its tyres and tubes	50.00
Webb for using its front forks	8.00
Teclemit for using its grease nipples	30.00
ACU prize money for winning the Junior TT	100.00
for winning the Junior TT	250.00
ACU prize money for second place in the Senior TT	70.00
Veloce Ltd for second place in the Senior TT	100.00

The grand total was a not inconsiderable £981.14.6, in addition to which Stanley Woods received the winnings and bonuses for all the other races he was involved in.

Woods was contracted to Veloce Ltd in 1938 to ride in four events – the Leinster 100, the North-West 200, the Ulster GP and the IOM TT – plus he had a full continental programme. He was clearly a superstar of his era, based on his annual income (the average UK income at that time was in the order of £200). It is perhaps with this in mind that Percy Goodman proposed that Stanley forego £200 of his retainer to fund the new 500cc racer that was being developed, in the likelihood that this loss would be made up in winning bonuses once the machine was put into competition. Thus, Stanley Woods is the only recorded contributor to the financing of the Roarer outside the Goodman family.

Up to the reconstruction of the Roarer it was considered that Woods was the only person who had ridden it in anger. This occurred at the 1939 TT when the Roarer, whilst still being developed, was taken for a demonstration lap around the Island. The recorded lap time was a slow 39 minutes (58mph average), due to the need to frequently change sparkplugs that could not cope with the combustion temperatures. A harder grade plug oiled up due to excess oil being delivered by the supercharger. The assumption that Stanley Woods was the only rider of the Roarer was, however, questioned in a letter received by Gordon Small, editor of *Classic Motorcycle Legends* in 1995 (*Classic Motorcycle Legends* No 34, Autumn 1995, page 40) from a Mr Cyril Scott of Cornforth. The text of this letter is reproduced below:

Stanley Woods with the Roarer at the 1939 TT.

Dear Gordon
You may care to mention to Ivan Rhodes that my old friend Billy Tiffin Jnr also rode the racer on the mountain during practice for the 1939 TT.
I have him on audio tape recalling the bike's wonderful smoothness. He said the factory was only testing its handling at the 1939 TT, and that both he and Stanley Woods thought it was equal to the high standard of the KTT in this respect.
With the supercharger on very low boost, he said the top speed was about the same as the works 500cc Velo singles, but that Veloce were very confident they would sort out the teething troubles, such as lubrication, for the 1940 season. With increased blower boost they would have the machine very competitive.

Billy Tiffin Jnr and his father had a Velocette agency in Carlisle, Cumbria, and were great friends of the Goodman family. Billy Jnr took part in the 1938 ISDT on a bike specially prepared for him. It is often recounted in local circles that he rode the Roarer in 1939 but, unfortunately, it has not been possible to verify the veracity of this claim.

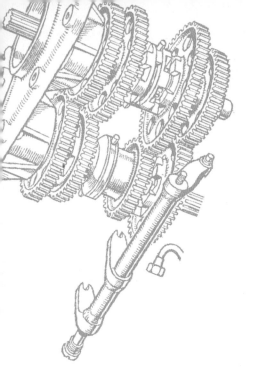

The motorcycles

Chapter 3

The Roarer

Introduction

Prior to 1938 the main opposition in the Senior TT had been Norton, but it was clear that motorcycle developments overseas, namely BMW and Gilera, would lead Veloce down the path of multi cylinders and supercharging if it was to claim the Senior TT trophy. Harold Willis took some time to consider the opposition before committing the company to a particular approach. Experience of Clara had revealed some of the potential problems of supercharging a single-cylinder engine. Interesting though they were, the supercharged singles of the 1930s were essentially conversions of existing bikes, with the supercharger attached wherever possible. If supercharging was to be exploited to the full, it was clear that motorcycle engines should follow the established practice of car and aero engine design in having the engine designed from scratch for supercharging. This was recognised by BMW which, in 1930, built a supercharged flat twin with the supercharger mounted above the gearbox, driven through the magneto shaft at half engine speed. This 500cc engine produced 55hp (41kW).

Subsequent development led, in 1935, to a front-mounted supercharger driven directly by the crankshaft to produce a boost pressure of 15psi (1 bar). With 68bhp (50.72kW) and weighing only 302lb (137kg), the supercharged BMW was very quick, capable of reaching 140mph (225km/hr), but handled badly. A string of distance records and record-breaking, together with GP victories for Karl Gall and Otto Ley, preceded a sixth place in the 1937 Senior TT, and victory for Jock West at the Ulster GP two months later.

In 1934 Rondine produced a transverse water-cooled four, supercharged by a Rootes-type 'blower' mounted above the gearbox and close coupled to the inlet manifold. Producing 60bhp (44.76kW), this design won its first competitive race, the 1935 Tripoli GP. Further development of the engine and cycle parts after the design was sold to Gilera raised peak power to 85bhp (63.4kW), and top speed to 145mph (233.3km/hr).

In England AJS displayed a V4 at the London Motor Show, which could be supplied with a blower in place of a dynamo, should the customer so desire. This design appeared in many manifestations, culminating in water-cooling, rear-facing exhausts on all cylinders and pannier oil tank. Maximum power was 80bhp (59.68kW): the bike was fast in a straight line but suffered from poor handling.

Harold Willis realised it was essential that the rider should be able to make full use of the power available from the engine. From his own racing experience he was very concerned about the amount of oil thrown onto the back tyre of a chain-driven bike, as this would limit cornering ability. He was in favour of shaft drive with the shaft enclosed within the swing arm, and, to eliminate power-sapping bevel gears at the input end of the driveshaft, a longitudinal driveline. Vertical cylinders were favoured because of the apparent vulnerability of the horizontal cylinders of the BMW.

Willis argued that the BMW's poor handling was due to gyroscopic precession of the inline crankshaft reacting to pitching of the bike, due to suspension movement, producing reactions that tended to cause yawing. His solution to these problems was radical and quite unique, developed from the application of first principles to the basic design. He chose to neutralise the forces by using two contra-rotating crankshafts geared together, effectively combining two vertical singles side-by-side in the frame, the gyroscopic forces produced by pitching during acceleration and braking being cancelled out within the crankcase. As an added bonus, the use of 100 per cent balance factor cancelled out the primary out of balance forces, leaving the low magnitude secondary as the only out of balance force. The use of two crankshafts was fortuitous also in that one crank could be connected to the gearbox and transmission, and the other could provide a drive for a supercharger and magneto.

The design

Veloce responded to the continental challenge of supercharging by disregarding all preconceived views of motorcycle design, and, starting from first principles with a clean sheet of paper, produced one of the most iconic designs in motorcycle engineering. The design originated from the fertile mind of Harold Willis in 1936, and the general arrangement **drawing**, dated 1937, demonstrates how far the concept had developed by that date, with liquid cooling, telescopic forks, and twin contra-rotating crankshaft with shaft drive enclosed in a torque tube forming the rear swing arm suspension. The heart of the machine is the twin contra-rotating crankshafts placed in-line and coupled through gears aft of the crankshafts.

Once this arrangement has been settled the integrity of the design then becomes evident. The port-side crank (as designated by Willis) provided the power output, whilst a centric supercharger was driven via the starboard crankshaft. The frame followed standard Velocette geometry with the centre of mass of the engine below the wheel spindles, which produced very stable roadholding. Power was transmitted via a Bendix constant velocity joint and driveshaft to a bevel box that also carried the rear brake. The rear wheel is dismountable by removing a dummy axle and distance piece, then displacing the wheel to the right to clear the brake shoes. The entire assembly of engine gearbox, transmission and rear wheel could be constructed as one unit (as per the integrated drivetrain invented much later by BMW with its K series bikes), onto which can be dropped the frame and forks.

Direction of primary and secondary forces with contra-rotating cranks.

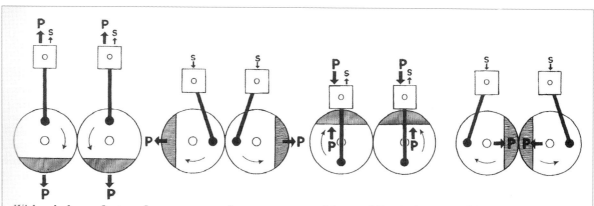

With a balance factor of 100 per cent, the contra-rotation of the crankshafts neutralises the primary inertia forces at both dead-centre positions, while the horizontal forces from the bobweights oppose one another at both mid-strokes

General arrangement drawing of the Roarer, 1937.

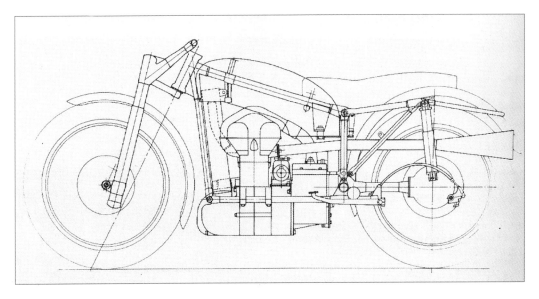

General arrangement drawing of the engine and gearbox. Apologies for the poor condition of this image: this is the only known copy of the drawing.

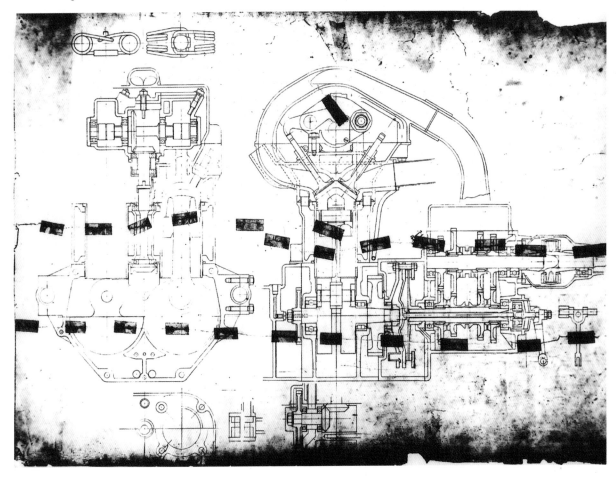

The frame and cycle parts

The frame of the Roarer is a complete departure from then-accepted Velocette practice. It can be considered to be formed in two distinct parts: a top piece that can be easily detached from the engine unit, and a lower part that remains attached to the engine. The concept is that of a space frame, with the engine acting as a stressed member to stiffen the whole assembly. A large diameter top tube runs from the steering head to where a saddle post would usually be. The heavily-gusseted steering head also locates two widely-spaced down tubes that fall each side of the engine. These are triangulated by two tubes located approximately one third and two thirds distance from the steering head, and which also carry the fuel tank mounts. The seat post is replaced by two widely-spaced tubes triangulated by a crosspiece above the swing arm pivot. This assembly is located at the top tube at a heavily-gusseted forging that also carries the seat mounting lug and locations for a triangulated rear subframe. As it stands, this arrangement has very weak torsional stiffness, but the frame is then completed by two horizontal longitudinal rails that attach to the front down tubes, and are fixed to the engine crankcase by two clamps on each side, and two mounting points at the rear. The engine itself is a stressed member that completes a very light and rigid assembly. Towards the rear of the

Engine and drive system assembled in the frame.

longitudinal rails are large brackets that contain the swinging arm bearings and mountings for the saddle support tubes and the lower parts of the rear subframe. The footbrake and gearchange levers are located at the end of the rails. Plain bushes are inserted into the swing arm bearing housing to bear stub axles that are integral with the swing arm.

Possibly at the insistence of Stanley Woods, the tried and tested Webb girder forks were used instead of the originally intended telescopic variety, and the rear suspension was provided by Dowty Oleomatic air-sprung oil-damped units. The brakes were of single leading shoe type and of 8-inch diameter: the rear brake being cable-operated, a diversion from usual Velocette practice.

A 21-inch aluminium wheel rim was laced into a full width hub, similar to those used on later Venoms, and shod with a 300 x 21 tyre. The rear wheel was of 19-inch diameter carrying a 3.25 x 19 tyre; also full width.

The hubs and brake drums were made in magnesium alloy treated with a suitable anti-corrosion coating.

The engine

The philosophy that exudes from the overall design is that of fitness for purpose. It is not clear from an external view, but many features of the KTT engine's design were used in the Roarer. Many of the cylinder head and crank assembly components are based on KTT practice, but a large proportion of the components are entirely new, indicating the degree of imaginative thought that went into this unique design. The main engine and transmission castings are in magnesium alloy of very stiff proportions. They are vertically split with heavily-ribbed bearing housings at each end. The vertical front and rear walls of the case, in which the massive main bearings are located, are in direct line, not only with the cylinder walls (as with the KTT) but also with the four lugs to which the engine is clamped to the bottom frame rails. The shafts are made of KE805, a direct oil-hardening or nitride-hardening high tensile nickel chrome steel that gives unrivalled wear and core strength properties. The crankshafts are very stiff with only $2^1/_{16}$in (52.38mm) between the inner faces of the main bearings.

Part-assembled cranks and crankcases.

The crankshafts are of bob weight type with the mainshafts forged integrally with the webs. The bob weights are relatively large to provide the 100 per cent balance factor, also reflected in the size of the main bearings. The crank pins are of $1^3/_8$in (34.925mm) in diameter, and shouldered so that, when pressed into the webs, the correct axial clearance is provided for the roller big ends.

The big end is of the caged roller type to prevent crowding of the rollers, and uses the standard Velocette roller bearing design of 16 rollers of $^3/_{16}$in (4.76mm) diameter and $^9/_{16}$in (14.28mm) length. These are contained in a duralumin cage with bars relieved on the inside to prevent contact with the roller track, and run directly on the forged and polished H-section steel connecting rods. The lack of an outer race reduced the overall width of the crank assembly, which is reflected in the overall width of the engine. When assembled, the minimum distance between the crank webs is only $^1/_{16}$in (1.5875mm).

Eight long studs extend from the top face of the crankcase to secure the one-piece cylinder block and the cylinder heads which are held in compression similar to the Mk 8 and the Mk 2 KSS. Hollow dowels are used to align the crankcase halves. To the rear of the crankcase is a chamber that houses the coupling gears. The gears are made from KE805 steel, cyanide hardened with stub teeth. These are located by Woodruff keys and pulled up against a taper on the mainshafts. Splines are machined on the centre bosses of the gears to provide couplings to the clutch centre on the port-side and the magneto and supercharger on the starboard-side. The crank arrangement does not feature flywheels as such but the combined inertia of the large bob weights and the crankshaft coupling gears is sufficient to ensure a smooth response to the throttle.

The cylinders are cast in a silicon-aluminium alloy chosen for its low thermal expansion rate, that required only 0.0015in (0.038mm) interference for the nickel cast iron liners which were dropped in cold while the block was at 100 degrees C. Bore size is 68mm and stroke 68.25mm, giving a swept volume of 496cc. At the front, driven off the starboard crank, a pair of spur gears provide drive to the oil pump and overhead cam located in the timing chest, which is closed at the front by the streamlined

Crankshaft components.

oil tank. The cam drive followed normal Veloce practice with shaft and bevel gears, the shaft running between the cylinders and engaging with an Oldham coupling to two sets of bevel gears. The top set of bevel gears terminate in a chamber colloquially known as 'the grandfather clock,' which is bolted to the cam boxes. The top bevel drives both camshafts, which act upon rockers pivoting on eccentric spindles for valve adjustment, an arrangement used on the Mk 8 KTT and the Mk 2 KSS. The ends of the rockers are Stellite-faced.

Cast in Y-alloy the cylinder head design is clearly based on the Mk 8 KTT, except that the rocker boxes are separate, not integral. Initially, Udall had proposed DOHC valve gear, but this was vetoed by Willis, who remembered the failure in the 1936 TT. The horizontal finning is roughly square viewed from above, and the fins between the valve spring wells are divided vertically to preclude thermal distortion of the exhaust valve seats. In the part spherical combustion chamber, the aluminium bronze exhaust valve seat and the nickel-manganese-chrome steel inlet valve seat are shrunk into the head material. Valve guides of aluminium bronze are cut flush with the roof of the inlet port. Sodium-cooled, the KE965 exhaust valves have chrome stems as a precaution against picking up in the guides. The overlapping hairpin valve springs are identical to those used in the Viper and Venom engines, and the two-piece top collars allow the valves to rotate freely. The cylinder head joint is a lapped spigot designed to minimise any tendency of the clamping pressure to taper the liner bores.

*The integrated
drivetrain
being
assembled.*

The long through-bolts that unite the crankcase elements and secure the head and barrels to the crankcase are waisted and polished to confer a degree of torsional flexibility and fatigue strength.

The pistons of RR59 alloy are machined all over; they have three compression rings and an oil scraper. The additional compression ring is intended to increase heat dissipation from the piston: this is quite normal for supercharged engines of this era. Additional oil cooling was also provided by oil flung under the piston crown from the big end bearings by rotation of the crankshafts. The pistons were diamond-turned tapered and oval to ensure a round and parallel shape when at running temperatures. Flats on the crown provide clearance for the valves, whilst surplus weight was shed by drilling blind holes above the gudgeon pin boss. To prevent flutter at high rpm the compression rings are of keystone section, ie tapered radially inward to reduce weight for a given radial depth, which determines the rate at which they absorb heat from the grooves.

The lubrication system is based on the well-tried KTT system in which oil is directed through calibrated jets of various sizes to the vital parts. Driven at one-third engine speed by a skew gear on the front of the port-side crankshaft, the gear-type oil pump lifted oil through a strainer in the bottom of the oil tank and forced it through a fine mesh filter into drillings in the tank rear wall. The pressurised oil is supplied to the big end bearings, and then by fling to the main bearings. External pipes with metering quills supply the valve gear and magneto drive gears. A jet at the rear end of a drilling on the crankcase centre line meters oil to the point of contact of the coupling gears. Oil accumulating in the sump flows through two large holes in the front crankcase wall, to be returned by a scavenge pump to an external oil tank. The tank is fitted with a froth tower and a quick-action filler cap.

The magneto drive is a very complicated piece of machining as the magneto is placed transversely at the rear of the cylinder, requiring a spiral and spur tooth drive in the coupling that also contains a shock absorber for the supercharger drive. A Centric sliding vane compressor provides the fuel air mixture via a $^{11}/_{16}$in (27mm) Amal carburettor. Initial thought was given to a Foxwell blower of the type used on Whiffling Clara, and admired by Willis for the support the design offered to the sliding vanes. Unfortunately, this also resulted in high friction losses that Udall did not tolerate.

Following an unsuccessful attempt to make his own blower based on the Foxwell design, Willis began discussions with Shorrocks, which gave Veloce a specification for a blower fitted to an MG car. Relations with Shorrocks became very close so that when this company merged with Centric the decision was taken to fit this type of blower.

In the original water-cooled conception the exhaust pipes were rearward-facing, with the inlet tract running from the supercharger, over the top of the engine to the forward-facing inlet ports. This arrangement was retained when air cooling was adopted as it was felt by Willis that rearward-facing exhaust pipes produced a power boost by reducing pumping losses. Willis was aware that the front wheel and mudguard masked the front of the engine from cooling air, so in the case of the singles, designed the large square cylinder heads with deep, highly conductive fins that

could penetrate the moving air stream around the bike to provide adequate cooling. Cooling of the cylinder head around the rearward-facing exhaust ports is very marginal, relying on the heat being conducted through the head material to a cooler region. Willis had a concern about the exhaust pipes on the Roarer over-heating, so side scoops were arranged to direct air onto the exhaust pipe, and, if necessary, an oil cooler could be added. The initial build used cams of KTT profile, but these were found to be unsuitable for a supercharged engine, which has a larger pressure differential between the exhaust and inlet gases. A large valve overlap is undesirable as it promotes a tendency for the high pressure incoming charge to be pumped across the

Roarer engine loosely assembled.

Magneto and supercharger drive coupling.

is light for a robust construction, and accurate manufacture made it possible to secure complete disengagement with only $1/16$in (1.5875mm) axial movement on the pressure plate.

The backplate of the clutch is driven by a splined muff coupling from the port-side coupling gear, and is secured by the same large nut that fastens the coupling gear to the port-side crank. Ten equally-spaced, high tensile steel studs, threaded at each end, are screwed into the backplate. The backplate is drilled with 20 holes, undercut to take thimbles, into which are placed the clutch springs. The springs press on to the first driving plate that is slipped over the ten studs. The friction plates and two remaining driving plates are then assembled and the springs brought into compression by nuts that are brought up against a shoulder on the threaded studs. The centres of the friction plates run on a splined coupling that is internally splined to engage with the gearbox input shaft. The first pressure plate is a complete disc with a pressure pad in the centre. The clutch is operated by a slender rod that passes through the hollow input shaft to press on the pressure pad and compress the springs. This then releases the clutch. Externally, the rod is pushed by a cable-operated bell crank located on the back of the gearbox that includes an adjustable thrust pin to take up slack to accommodate bedding in of the clutch plates. The pressure required to operate the clutch (which is very light) is controlled by the length of the actuation arm of the bell crank. Lubrication is fed to the clutch release mechanism via a radial drilling on the input shaft.

The four-speed, constant mesh, all-indirect gearbox is as unusual as the clutch; the required vertical offset to align the gearbox output shaft with the bevel box is achieved by using large diameter, liberally-drilled gears. As the input shaft runs at engine speed, the peripheral and engagement speeds of the gears are high, but this is offset by the low tooth loading that this brings about, so the gears are very narrow by contemporary motorcycle standards.

Beginning at the clutch the order of the gear pairs is 4th, 1st, 2nd and 3rd. 4th and 3rd gears on the input shaft are free to rotate on the shaft on needle roller bearings located by a shoulder and the bearing. 1st and 2nd gears form a sliding gear that runs along a splined section of

combustion chamber and out through the still closing exhaust valve.

Clutch and gearbox

With a twin-cylinder engine the clutch has to cope with the maximum torque of one of the cylinders acting alone; in this case a cylinder of 250cc capacity. A suitable design can be achieved in several ways to provide the required area of friction material for a specified contact pressure. In the case of the BMW, a large diameter single plate clutch is used, but for the Roarer the space available dictated a small diameter multi plate-type. The clutch, which is dry and ventilated, has 7 plates and 20 springs, giving a total clamping pressure of 500lbf (2.24kN). The clutch operation the shaft. The external faces of the sliding gear are dog clutches that engage with the 3rd and 4th gear wheels when required, making them effectively fixed to the shaft when engaged. A similar arrangement is found on the output shaft, with 3rd and 4th gears being pressed on splines, making them fixed to rotate with the shaft. 1st and 2nd gears, located on the shaft by a shoulder, and 3rd and 4th gear wheels also run on needle roller bearings.

Between these gears is a sliding dog that engages the drive when required. In order to engage 1st gear the sliding dog on the output shaft engages with the 1st gear pinion, permitting the drive to go from the input shaft, through the 1st gear pair of gears and then to the output shaft. 4th gear is engaged by moving the sliding gear on the input shaft to lock the 4th gear to the input shaft, so that the drive now goes from the input shaft, through the 4th gear pair and into the output shaft. Control of the sliding gear and dog is achieved by a pair of selector forks positioned by a cam plate located on the top of the gearbox. The particular arrangement of the gear pairs on the shafts, which is different to the usual Velocette arrangement, requires only one track on the cam plate. A conventional foot change mechanism completes the gear selection components.

The gearbox case incorporates a removable panel held on eight studs that can be removed to assist assembly of the gear mechanisms. The castings of the crankcases, coupling gear housing, clutch housing and gearbox are pulled together by long studs running through hollow dowels for location. A steel reinforcing plate is located at the rear of the gearbox and the supercharger, which relieves the castings of load and also serves as the rear mounting to the frame.

The reinforcing steel plate at the rear of the gearbox.

*Gearbox
with internals
and selector
mechanism,
and mounting
for the
supercharger.*

Final drive

The reasons Harold Willis chose shaft drive for the Roarer are many faceted. His main concern was the oil that was flung onto the back tyre of a chain-driven bike over a long race distance. Having placed the crankshafts in line with the frame, it naturally followed that the place for a bevel gear to turn the drive across the frame is at the rear wheel spindle. Finally, although the efficiency of a bevel gear is lower than that of a new chain, the bevel box retains its efficiency over a large mileage while a chain can deteriorate to the point of breaking. Consider also that the high strength steels used today for chains were not available when the Roarer was laid down, so chain wear and breakage was common.

The driveshaft originally included a rubber coupling behind the gearbox, developed by Hardy Spicer. This was tried and seems to have worked very well. At some stage, however, this was changed to a Bendix Weiss Constant Velocity (CV) joint. Perhaps mindful of the failure of the driveshaft coupling on the DOHC engine, the idea was to relieve the Roarer driveshaft of torsion stresses that would be produced by a universal joint when the suspension moved. It is possible that this change was instigated by Hardy Spicer, which could have been an agent for Bendix. The driveshaft is waisted as opposed to being hollow, as the latter design would be much stiffer in torsion, although lighter, perhaps. The driveshaft runs in the offside of the swinging arm suspension unit with the CV joint inline with the

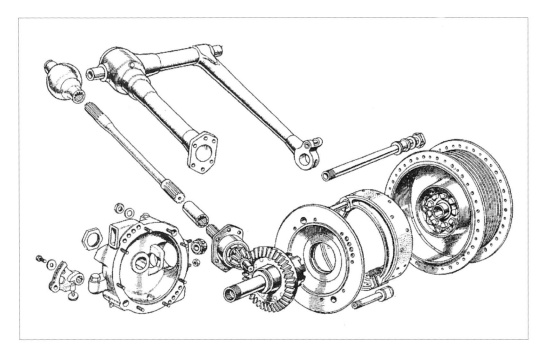

Final drive, swing arm, driveshaft with CV joint and bevel box.

suspension pivots. The swing arm unit is a steel fabrication with locations for the frame pivots and for mounting the bevel box, and serves also as a torque tube to resist the reaction force of the crown wheel. As mentioned earlier, the driveshaft is waisted, with splines cut at each end to engage with the CV joint and the splined shaft of the final drive by way of a muff coupling. A gear ratio of 3.777:1 in the bevel box was achieved with a tooth ratio of 34:9.

As the port-side crankshaft rotates in an anti-clockwise direction (viewed from the front), the crown wheel of the bevel box is inboard of the driveshaft. The crown wheel shaft is hollow and rotates around a fixed inner sleeve fixed into the outer casing of the bevel box. The inner end of the crown wheel shaft has teeth that engage with similar teeth formed on the wheel hub, which is in one piece with the brake drum. In installing the rear wheel, the hub is slid into place and retained by a substantial spindle that passes through the starboard-side rear fork end through a distance piece and the hub, and is screwed into the inner sleeve already mentioned. When the rear wheel is removed, the rear brake shoes and operating mechanism are left in place.

The rotating components are liberally drilled, with the intention of reducing overall weight of the bike, but, at 370lb (167kg) dry, it is still some

50lb (22.65kg) heavier than a Mk 8 KTT.

Building was completed in the spring of 1939, when Stanley Woods displayed the Roarer at the Isle of Man during TT practice. In this form it had 3.945psi (0.272 bar) boost pressure and a $^{15}/_{16}$in (23.8mm) carburettor. Although no more power was produced than that from the 500 single, the smooth contours of the engine and integral oil tank boosted top speed by 6mph (9.6km/hr) to 130mph (209km/hr). Woods was delighted with the superb handling, silky smooth running and broad spread of power – from 2000rpm to 7000rpm against 4500 to 6700 for the single. There seemed to be plenty of room for improvement and, with a whole winter ahead for further development, Charles Udall began the search for more power.

Udall began by not driving the blower directly from the crankshaft; boost pressure was increased to 13psi (0.884 bar), and the cylinder compression ratio lowered from 8.75:1 to 7.5:1. Carburettor size was changed to $1^{1}/_{16}$in (27mm), and the valve timing stretched. Within two months, net power output had increased to 54bhp (40.28kW).

With hindsight it is possible to consider what might have happened if Willis had not died and war been declared in 1939. Would an extra year of development and the technical flair of Willis

Percy Goodman astride the Roarer in 1939.

the engine was initially conceived, the intention was to use liquid cooling, but this was changed to conform to the factory policy of making the racing and production products identifiable, one with the other. Of the energy that enters an engine (the chemical energy stored in the fuel), approximately one third is used to produce power, with the remaining two thirds dissipated through external cooling and carried away in the exhaust gases in equal measure.

The hottest parts of the engine are usually the exhaust valve – which has a very difficult life – and the region of the cylinder head around this valve. These hotspots can give rise to detonation if the temperature of the unburnt fuel and air mixture increases to a point where pre-flame reactions can occur. The resulting shock within the combustion chamber causes excessive bearing loads, and dramatically increases the heat transfer rate to the cylinder walls. Remember, this was at a time before high octane fuels had been developed, and the importance of combustion chamber geometry in reducing quench zones and short flame paths was not fully understood. The heat-resistant steel alloys that were developed for gas turbine production were not available in 1939, so the performance of exhaust valves was marginal, with detached heads a common occurrence. The high internal temperatures produced by supercharging and running for long periods at full power would have caused problems in these areas if sufficient cooling was not provided around the exhaust valve. It is likely that a return to liquid cooling would have been necessary as output power was increased with continuous development. When asked by Titch Allen if the Roarer would have been a TT winner, Phil Irving responded with: "Only if it had been liquid-cooled." The weight penalty could have been overcome, and the superior roadholding inherent in the design would have been a great advantage, if only the machine had been robust and reliable.

The Roarer was displayed around Velocette dealers for several years as an exhibition piece; it was this activity that resulted in the internals being removed and stored in the race shop as the reduced weight made handling easier. The internals inevitably deteriorated as their container was used as a nest by a family of rats.

On closure of the factory, the bike – along with the Model O, the 24 hour record-breaker,

have produced a senior TT victory for Veloce? The opinion of the authors is probably not in the first incarnation. Two factors were against this: weight and inadequate cooling. The complexity of the design, with two crankshafts and coupling gears, produced a heavy bike. The frame is lighter than a Mk 8 frame due to the use of welded joints instead of brazed joints with malleable lugs, but the steel petrol tank is very heavy (this could have been replaced by an aluminium version as these became popular, post-war).

Post-1939 TT development that increased power output to 54bhp (40.28kW) was achieved by driving the compressor independently from the crankshaft at a significantly higher speed than the crankshaft. To modify the compressor drive to include a step-up gear, possible epicyclical, would have required a major redesign in this area of the engine, or a redesign of the compressor. When and the TT winners were sold to journalist John Griffith, who put them on display in the Stanford Hall motorcycle museum. On inspection, it was confirmed that the internals – including the crankshafts, gears, oil pump and other items – were missing, but a pair of pistons was in the bores. John Griffith exhausted all lines of enquiry trying to locate the original parts without success, so eventually considered remanufacturing them. Whether the internals could have been saved during the factory liquidation sale is debatable, but the very special CV joint was recovered and given to John. Sadly, John Griffith was killed in a motor accident in 1975 before work could get fully under way.

Fast forward now to 1982 when John Griffith's sons, Stephen and David, were considering selling the Roarer. They had received very generous offers from a Japanese concern, but considered that Ivan Rhodes was the only person who could restore the bike to running condition. A price below the Japanese offer was agreed, with terms that allowed Ivan to raise the cash by building and selling on some vintage bikes from his collection.

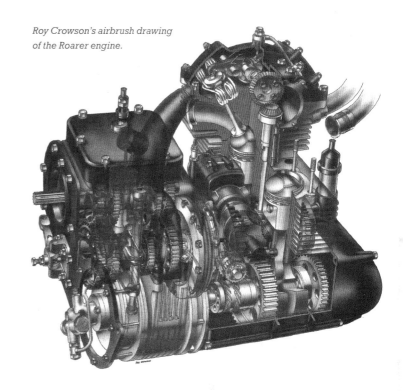

Roy Crowson's airbrush drawing of the Roarer engine.

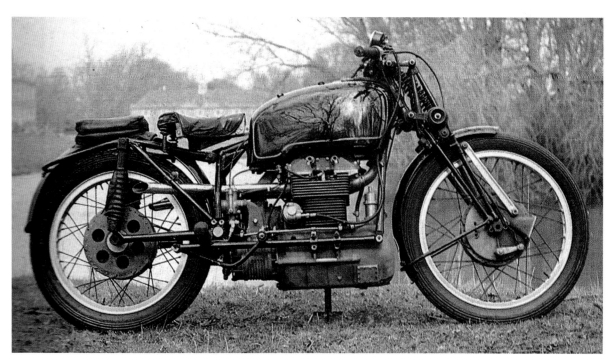

The Roarer at Stanford Hall after leaving the factory. The chrome exhaust pipes and lack of deflectors denote an engine devoid of internals.

Ivan's account of the Roarer rebuild

It was probably the first of the Belle Vue shows, forerunner of the Stafford Show, initially set up by Alan Whitehead when Stanley Woods was guest of honour. 1980, I think it was, and Stephen Griffith – whose family owned the Roarer at that time – was requested to get it assembled, the bike having been lying around in a dismantled state for a while, though normally it had been on display at the Stanford Hall Museum in Leicestershire.

The machine was presented in oily rag condition for Stanley's interviews for the press and television, I believe. We knew Stanley quite well by this time, having provided him with what we now call 'Stanley's Big Velo' for demonstration at various venues: Malloy and Donington, and, of course, laps of honour in the Isle of Man.

Whilst at the show I dropped a hint to Stephen Griffith that perhaps he should sell us the Roarer; after all, it contained no internals, which meant that to get it up and running would require much effort and expense, and I think perhaps the seed was sown. Stephen was aware that we had resurrected two of the works 500s from the remnants of the old race shop, in order that Stanley and Bill Lomas could complete the laps in the inaugural occasion in June 1979, and eventually responded with the comment that since we had come up with the goods with these other two, we stood a good chance of handling this one! A price was agreed and paid over a 12 month period when other machines were built and sold off to provide the necessary funds.

Once home, a plan had to be implemented, so we invited the Jones twins – Dennis Jones and his twin, Glyn, both engineers and friends, and quite local to us, too – round for discussion.

There were no drawings available, so as much information as possible was sought, and a certain amount of material came in the form of a GA drawing given to me by Brian in 1969, with a detailed exploded drawing produced for The Motor Cycle *magazine (preparation of the exploded drawing may explain why the engine was dismantled). This was so well done that Grahame, when producing the working drawings, found such detail was most helpful in achieving the accuracy required.*

We required forgings for crankshafts and coupling gears, and it was suggested that we contact Brian Scully in Sheffield, who had been responsible for such items to produce the Matt Holder 350 Scott, quite apart from being its development rider. His advice gave us an introduction to a small forging company in Sheffield, which came up with the hand-forged goods, enabling us to make a start.

I was chasing around the countryside in those days selling process equipment to industry on behalf of William Boulton of Burslem, Stoke- on-Trent, namely deburring and vibro finishing equipment to companies making cutlery in Sheffield, turbine blades and NGVs at Rolls-Royce, and a variety of other concerns usually connected with the motor industry.

Grahame – who, by this time, had joined George Silk in Derby as an apprentice – was conversant with a range of machine tooling, some of which we subsequently acquired when George updated to C&C, which gave us a big Dean &Grace lathe and a Halifax external grinder, and a milling machine that I recall we bought from GEC Wheatstone in Leicestershire.

Ex-Veloce works director Peter Goodman had set up Goodman Gears, thus enabling continuity of manufacture of all the Veloce gearbox internals, the tooling of which eventually passed to Dave Holder of the Velocette Company. Peter cut the two 1 inch wide coupling gears and provided the necessary jig for critical dimensions. For clutch plates we contacted our good friends at W A Tyzak Ltd of Sheffield, who provided pieces from the scrap bin: EN41 I think it was, which we took home for machining with the promise that Tyzak would broach a suitably-sized centre when an opportunity arose.

Grahame made a hub to suit which located on the gearbox input shaft.

The clutch plates requiring inserts came from other friends, Sheepbridge Sintered Products of Sutton in Ashfield, who gave us the latest technology sintered bronze coatings as used on racing cars to this day.

We met up with Charles Udall who, from his personal notebook, gave us the details of the tooth form and angles of the skew gear that drove, via a muff coupling, the magneto drive. This also incorporated a shock absorber, carrying a number of Veloce clutch springs, to the blower drive. We could not find a gear-cutting company with the facility to handle the skew gear due to the excessive angle of 67 degrees of the teeth, but eventually found Rolls-Royce, Bristol was using a machine that could do it. This, however, was in constant use making parts for the Bristol Pegasus engine, with little chance of a gap in production in the foreseeable future.

We had some months before helped out Rolls-Royce, Derby by vibro-finishing all its production blades for a period of four months, all to a revised spec, thus enabling completion of an order in a limited time that otherwise could have resulted in penalty clauses being invoked. On completion, the Engineering Director stated that, should I need a favour in future, I was only to ask ... this done, we had two sets of finished skew gears within a week and were able to continue.

The reconstruction

Upon acquiring the Roarer, the enormity of the task ahead of Ivan became apparent. Dismantling the bike had revealed that the gearbox was complete but the clutch was missing, as was the oil pump, the drive to the blower and magneto, and all but one bevel for the cam drive. Fortunately, the motor contained the pistons pushed into the bores and one head had the valves and springs in place. The two crankshafts were missing, along with the connecting rods. The crankshaft coupling gears, the camshaft drive gear, the oil pump drive, and the camshafts (which are handed) were all missing. Luckily, the vertical driveshaft to the cams, which had one of the bottom bevels on it and is a special, was in place in the tube between the cylinder bores.

At an early stage Ivan called a meeting of everyone he thought would be able to assist in the project. Amongst those who attended were Dennis Jones, his brother, Glen, and Ivan's two sons, Grahame and Adrian. At the time, Grahame was working for George Silk of Derby of Scott fame, where much of the machining of components was undertaken. Eventually, Ivan arranged to swop with George a deburring machine for a surplus big lathe and an external grinding machine, thus bringing the machining work to Fellside. At first, the engine castings were studied: no drawings existed, apart for some of Charles Udall's sketches and rough arrangements, and an article written by Vic Willoughby with an exploded drawing of the engine and transmission by Frank Beak from *The Motor Cycle* of 1957. A set of drawings was eventually produced and contact made with Charles Udall, whose carefully preserved notebooks proved invaluable.

The engine and gearbox castings were now freed up to be bead-blasted and X-ray crack tested: amazingly, all of the castings passed with flying colours. These were then subjected to dichromate corrosion inhibition and coating in phenolic resin to ensure they were totally free of porosity, then painted matte black. Almost every internal component had to be re-created. Several items required specialist machining processes beyond the capabilities of the home workshop: one such component was the ingenious combined supercharger and magneto power take-off. This incorporated a shock absorber plus a skew gear to turn the magneto drive through 90 degrees, so that the magneto could be mounted across the top of the crankcase. The shock absorber isolated the supercharger from shock loading, which it could not tolerate. Eight little conical plungers with clutch springs behind (similar to a Vincent output shaft shock absorber designed by Phil Irving) engaged with detents in the blower drive hub. The hub is retained on the blower shaft by a taper and special nut which has a locking plate to prevent it coming loose. Charles Udall advised that he took this design from the dynamo drive of his MG J2. The only place in the UK that could machine this complicated part was the Rolls-Royce factory in Bristol, which cut such gears for the Bristol Pegasus turbine engine.

After the blanks had been left with Rolls-Royce for over a year with no progress due to pressure to meet production orders, as mentioned previously, Ivan reminded Rolls-Royce management that he had saved the company some five million pounds in penalty payments when the production RB211 failed to meet the guaranteed performance. A finishing process developed at Rolls-Royce, called RPS619 super finishing, which has become standard procedure at Rolls-Royce, was successfully applied by Ivan to the turbine blades of the new engine, enabling the company to achieve the guaranteed performance and deliver the engines on time without penalty. Top management was very grateful to Ivan and told him: "If we can do anything to help, just ask."

The oil pump was another item that caused some head-scratching. The engine would need more oil than the 350 single due to the proliferation of moving parts. The pump was sandwiched between the forward mounted oil chamber and the crankcase, which, when placed together, hide the pump so that it is not possible to inspect the area to determine pump size. The oil was delivered to the highly loaded parts such as the camshaft and bevel gears, etc. Two cylinders meant twice as many jets compared to a single, so there are seven jets compared to three on a Mk 8. The Frank Beak drawing of the engine gave the impression that the pump was like that used on Nortons, though no such pump could be persuaded to fit, so endless calculations and drawings were produced before a special body was made to house a set of gears twice the width of those used on a Mk 8.

Pump speed was another problem. The drive was a worm and wheel arrangement. A photo of works mechanic Tommy Mutton dismantling the engine in 1956 showed the oil pump on a bench in the background. Using a powerful magnifying glass, Ivan was almost able to see the number of starts of the driving worm. One third engine speed for the pump was decided on, as on the Venom 500cc bike that uses a similar type of drive.

Whilst this was going on, the cycle parts were checked through and refurbished in the traditional black with genuine gold leaf transfers and tank lining. The original rev counter was despatched to Dennis Quinlin in Australia for refurbishment. Dennis raced a Mk 8 in classic

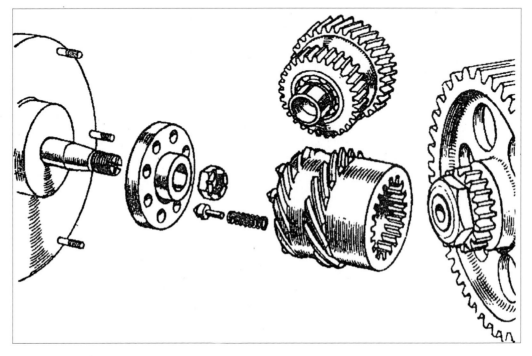

Magneto and supercharger drive coupling.

races, and hosts a web blog site – Velobangogent – which is full of Velocette tales and pictures.

The drawing by Frank Beak proved very useful when work began on the clutch, as it provided information such as the number of studs, lightening holes, etc. Clutch plates were obtained from W A Tyzack Ltd, manufacturer of clutch plates, and an old established customer of Ivan's. On a visit there it was found that material in the scrap bin was the right diameter for the Roarer plates, and that a recent order from America would be using the same size broach, so the Roarer plates were stacked with the American job and, hey presto! 15 clutch plates to size and broached were the result. The splined hub for the clutch plates was made to suit the broaching, which is not exactly the same as the original used by Veloce. The internal splines are the same as those in a Velocette gearbox.

The driven plates were taken to Sheepbridge Sintered products of Sutton-in-Ashfield, another old customer of Ivan's, to be surfaced with a sintered bronze friction material. Sheepbridge was also able to offer advice on spring pressures. The dimensions of the ten studs that transmit the drive from the body to the driving plates were arrived at after initial assembly. Both driving and driven plates, plus the pressure plate, are manufactured from EN24T steel. The outer face of the clutch body was marked with degrees to facilitate valve and ignition timing, as was done originally.

A trip to Germany on business arranged by an old friend, Dr Helmut Krackawitzer, saw Ivan at the Mahle piston factory, where he obtained three sets of new pistons using the originals as patterns. The supercharger was also taken along as it had bad score marks in the housing caused by stones, which must have entered through the carburettor when Stanley Woods demonstrated the Roarer at the TT circuit. Mahle coated the interior of the supercharger with a nickasil process and restored the original surface.

The top vertical bevel driving the two camshafts is the same as on the works motors running on ball bearings. This is somewhat different to the KTT, in which the top bevel runs a slightly smaller diameter plain bush. Fortunately, Ivan had several sets of these bevels, but the bottom bevel of the timing gears was a special and had to be made.

The first loose assembly of the components

began in 1988, and it went together beautifully, so it was decided to proceed to assembly with a test in mind. Many fiddly parts, such as the seal around the CV joint in the driveshaft, had to be made by hand and lapped in as this was the only way of retaining the oil in the gearbox and driveshaft area.

The moment of first firing occurred on 7 May, 1989 at Fellside. A party of assembled guests included Stanley Woods, Peter Goodman, Len Udall (brother of Charles and a race mechanic at Veloce in 1939), and Bill Udall (son of Charles who, unfortunately, was unable to be present).

Stanley Woods was in his element, his mind and memory as sharp as ever, recalling his ride on the Roarer at the Isle of Mann almost 50 years earlier.

The brief run given to the Roarer caused some concern about lubrication, as oil pressure dropped to 5psi when the engine warmed up. A trip to Cadwell Park for further testing on 17 May

Roarer: note rev counter.

Ivan and Grahame at Fellside, 7 May, 1989.

confirmed this. A lack of pressure from the blower was also evident. Handling was very precise but it was not possible to gauge power output. The high gearing to suit the TT circuit made the bike difficult to ride in slow corners, and also to obtain an accurate assessment of power. The Roarer is geared for 145mph (233km/hr) at 7000rpm, so being an all gear and shaft drive, it's not possible to change the gearing except by making a new final drive bevel box or altering gearbox ratios. At this time the cam fitted was based upon a Mk 8 KTT with full racing overlap. Udall's notes had recorded most power was obtained with this cam, but Ivan did not appreciate at the time that the blower had been driven independently at considerably more than crankshaft speed to produce 12psi (0.816 bar) boost. The low boost pressure and long overlap of the cam ensured that most of the charge was passing through the engine into the exhaust pipe.

The next outing was at the TT course where the Roarer was displayed alongside the 1939

Senior TT-winning BMW of George Meier, and the 1939 V4 AJS. These supercharged bikes took part in the Classic Lap for historic TT machines. All was going well until at the approach to Ballacraine, 8 miles (12.87km) out, Grahame felt the motor start to tighten up. Back at Fellside a stripdown revealed that one of the big ends had nipped sideways on to the cheek of the crank, the result of a too close clearance at the sides of the conrod big end eye. As it is a pressed-up fit, with the crank the same radius as the big end eye at this point, Grahame had to make some special tooling to split the two halves of the crank. This done, the surfaces were cleaned and a little more clearance introduced. At this time the camshaft was changed to one resembling a Mk 4 KTT cam (K17/6) with reduced valve overlap, that, on testing, showed an improvement in boost pressure to 5psi (0.34 bar), and also produced a sharper exhaust note.

The following is an extract from Ivan's diary that indicates the background to the public demonstration of the Roarer. It is taken from *Classic Motorcycle Legends No 10*.

May 7th, 1989. *The rebuilt Roarer is fired up and driven for the first time in public.*

May 19th, 1989. *Using the rolling road facilities at Paul Slater's Micron exhaust factory, the carburation is set up as the engine is run for around two hours under a variety of loading. The supercharger rebuilt with advice from Dieter Hertz shows zero pressure. There is no sign of the 4psi (0.272 bar) from 1939.*

May 23rd, 1989. *Now at Cadwell. Still no boost but the engine is almost uncannily smooth, and the handling is excellent. We all try it. It's over-geared, but, being shaft driven, nothing can be done. But we are grateful to Cadwell.*

May 30th, 1989. *We set out for the Island. The lack of boost pressure warrants a stripdown and an inspection but there is no time.*

June 1st, 1939. *At Jurby all seems well. We must go for the lap despite being marginally down on oil pressure.*

June 2nd, 1989. *We fill the bike with hot oil and Grahame finds it full of promise passing the BMW. It flew through Union Mills, sounding superb, but the motor tightened up at Ballacraine. Disappointed but not unduly surprised.*

June 4th, 1989. *Stripdown at home reveals no damage other than a slight nip of the big end outer ring between the flywheels on the right-hand crank. Everything else okay. Obviously needs more oil. There is sufficient material in the intricate and expensive oil pump body to increase the gear width. Pump speed is okay. Seven jets are fed from the single pump. We may need a bias to ensure a copious flow through the big ends. Reduce the amount of oil jetted into the coupling gears. Not so many options for the supercharger, which is fixed at engine speed. Its driving gear cannot be increased in size so think of closer tolerances. One other option was taken up by BMW in 1939. They told few people about it, and it involved a lot of work. But we may try that also. We are optimistic that we'll get it right.*

The lack of oil pressure was a concern. The width of the gears was increased by 50 per cent and the drive gear ratio changed to drive the pump at half engine speed. Ivan and Graham were now considering whether the oiling system design was fundamentally flawed from the outset, a view underpinned by a chance meeting with former works race mechanic Jack Passant, who confirmed that the motor had been marginal on the oil system whilst testing. It was thought that insufficient oil was entering the pump to maintain the pressure. In a single-cylinder Velocette the oil tank is mounted above the oil pump and connected by a large bore pipe that ensures a full supply, and provides an above-atmospheric inlet pressure. In the case of the Roarer, however, the oil pump is located at the bottom of the oil tank and connected by a small diameter hole. Careful enlargement of this hole – and reducing all sharp corners to create as good a flow path as possible – solved the problem, as subsequently a pressure of 12psi (0.816 bar) could be maintained when hot.

Upon investigating the lack of boost pressure it was discovered that the supercharger rotor

Left and overleaf: The Roarer at the Brands Hatch Festival of 1000 Bikes.

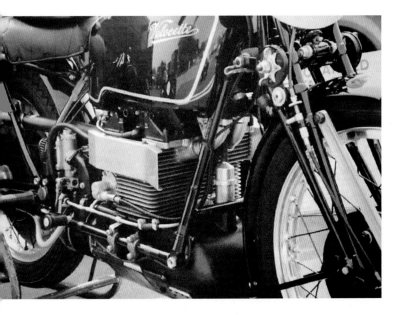

had been misaligned on manufacture by 0.10 inch; when this was corrected, satisfactory boost pressure was achieved.

The Roarer has appeared at many race meetings, and had many outings in the UK and abroad, without further distress, much to the delight of the many Velocette enthusiasts. In 1992, the giant Scania Motor Transport Company recognised this with its Scania Transport Trust Awards Scheme, which makes awards principally to museums or groups for major projects such as an aircraft or a ship. The Roarer project was put forward for entry by Brian Woolley, who wrote an article on the project for *Classic Motor Cycle,* and became one of the ten finalists. In September 1993, the Roarer was placed fourth, the worthy winner being a canal preservation group that had restored 90 miles (144km) of canal in the south of England.

Table 3.1 Specifications of the Roarer

Velocette 500 cc the Roarer 1936-39	
Type of engine	Supercharged four-stroke twin-cylinder geared cranks SOHC
Cylinders	Two-cylinder, 68 x 68.25mm, capacity 497.7cc
Compression ratio	7.5:1 with 13psi boost from the supercharger
Output bhp	54 @ 7000rpm
Valve system	SOHC, spur, bevel gears and shaft driven by starboard-side mainshaft
Ignition	Magneto, 14mm sparkplugs
Engine lubrication system	Dry sump, separate oil tank at front of crankcase
Oil pump	Double gear
Carburettor	Amal $1^1/_{16}$
Clutch	3-plate Veloce
Gearbox, primary and secondary drive	
Number of gears	4
Bevel box ratios	3.777:1, 34:9
Final drive	Enclosed shaft in swing arm with CV joint at suspension pivot
Frame, suspension and wheels	
Frame type	Welded tubes heavily-gusseted at steering head
Front suspension	Webb girder friction-damped
Rear suspension	Oleo pneumatic spring damper units
Brakes front, diameter, width, in	8
Brakes, rear, diameter, width, in	8
Rim sizes in	21 front, 19 rear
Tyre sizes in	300 x 21 front, 350 x 19 rear
Dimensions	
Unladen weight lb	370
Fuel tank capacity imp gall	$4^1/_2$
Oil tank capacity imp pt	8
Top speed mph	145

The Model O

Introduction

It was always Veloce's hope and intention that the knowledge gained from racing activities would lead to improvements in the production motorcycles. The factory specials were, to some extent, mobile test beds that allowed new ideas to be tried and tested and lessons learnt, and then introduced to the production range. Such was the soundness of the new K engine when it was introduced that it soon gained a reputation for first-rate performance and reliability, coupled with the capability of being performance tuned. It soon gained a following of privateers, and Alec Bennett was so impressed by the new design that he made an offer Percy Goodman couldn't afford to turn down, to be paid only if Bennett won the 1926 Junior TT with the new engine.

Initially, the basic models were developed for racing, but eventually a range of bikes evolved using the same engines and running gear, from the basic model (K) to the super sports (KSS) and the factory replica (KTT), to cater for all price ranges and performance levels. The Mk 2 KSS was developed from the racing machines. It can be argued that the Mk 2 KSS cylinder head was actually intended for the Mk 6 KTT, as a drawing now in Australia produced in 1934 and annotated Mk 6 clearly shows the head of the Mk 2 KSS.

Perhaps Willis' decision to use this head on the Mk 6 was not as arbitrary as was thought …

Veloce was very much a pioneer in motorcycle development. It is well known that the inventive mind of Willis conceived of the positive stop foot gearchange mechanism, and the dual seat (Loch Ness Monster) was another of his contributions. Frame and suspension design is another area that has benefited from Veloce input. A special frame was built in 1928 using Bentley and Draper patents, with a triangulated tubular swinging fork rear suspension, christened 'Spring Heel Jack' by Willis. In practice, it was found that the lower front ends of the fork assembly grounded under certain conditions so the idea was not taken further. Later, under Stanley Woods' guidance, the swing arm suspension system that is so familiar today was developed for the works racing bikes with Oleomatic oil-air suspension. During the 1930s, several European manufacturers were marketing bikes with pressed steel frames, which were cheaper to manufacturer and lighter than those fabricated using tube brazed into malleable castings.

Veloce inevitably showed an interest in pressed bodies for motorcycles. In his biography, Phil Irving describes a project he was working on in 1937 based on an MSS, that involved constructing an all-new pre-fabricated tail section. This was achieved by cutting off the rear section of a normal frame, and attaching to this by four bolts a

The Experimental MSS with rear fabricated frame section.

The Model O frame exposed.

hand-beaten pre-fabricated tail section designed to include adjustable (for load and damping) rear suspension. The method of adjustment by moving the spring damper units in arcuate slots was patented by Veloce Ltd and Irving (patent numbers 511875, 521106, 521107), and featured on all subsequent singles and the LE. Although not pretty, the arrangement worked very well. The spring damper units in this case consisted of a two-piece telescopic central stem kept in line with two Ferobestos bushes. Between the bushes a split Ferobestos sleeve was expanded against the outer sliding tube by a circular steel spring, so providing a suitable amount of friction damping.

Eugene Goodman was very interested in this development as a means of reducing the man hours involved in making conventional frames, as the stressed skin structure that enclosed the rear wheel could also contain built-in boxes for the battery and tool kit. After exhaustive tests of the prototype, it would seem it became factory policy to pursue this type of construction for future models, resulting in a purchase order for a large Lake Erie press in 1937.

The philosophy of racing improving the breed was also adopted when the Roarer was laid out.

Much of the design of the racer was undertaken by Charles Udall in the Racing Department, but at the same time Phil Irving was charged with laying out the drawings and producing a prototype road version of the same basic design; common features being an inline twin with contra-rotating cranks and shaft drive to a Quickly Detachable (QD) rear wheel. This became the Model O. These are about the only features that the Model O has in common with the Roarer as they were designed for different purposes: the Roarer an out-and-out racer designed for continued high speed running, demanding robustness and stamina; the Model O a fast touring machine of high quality. The Roarer is a hand-built thoroughbred with expense a secondary concern; the Model O was designed for mass production, with many features common in car manufacturing practice adopted to reduce costs and assembly time, and facilitate ease of maintenance.

The frame and cycle parts

The frame for the Model O is based on the geometry of the MSS, having the same head angle and front fork trail. Of duplex cradle form to the rear of the gearbox, whence are bolted a stressed skin tail section, similar to but much more elegant than that of the prototype sprung MSS.

The down tubes run from the malleable iron head lug at an angle of 20 degrees to a point just above the front engine lugs, then curve backwards to run alongside the sump to end at the lower rear corner lugs at the back of the gearbox. Two vertical down tubes run between the saddle lug and the corner lugs, from which short tubes extend rearward to carry folding pillion footrests. A cam action roll-on centre stand is attached to the corner lugs, which also contain two grease-lubricated bronze bushes for the rear fork pivot bearings. The rear forks consist of tubes brazed in a hollow malleable casting, formed with two dependent bosses to carry the hardened steel pivot pins retained by concealed nuts. The driveside tube carries a lug, bolted at two places to the bevel box, and also drilled for the frame spring attachment. To resist longitudinal torque reactions a stay is included between the bevel box and the pivot lug. The left-hand side is similar, the tube merely ending in a lug with holes for the pull-out axle and the frame spring. The rear portion of the frame is a fabricated stressed skin construction that incorporates the adjustable rear suspension, and also contains compartments for tools and battery storage.

The rear of the fabricated section is hinged to allow rear wheel removal. Rear suspension is via adjustable friction damped springs that have internal spring-damped Ferobestos bushes to provide friction damping, a setup that had been used on the experimental MSS and by Franz Binder in the 1939 TT. The springs are partly hidden by covers and can be adjusted by means of a pair of serrated hand wheels. The QD wheels are 19in front and rear and are interchangeable.

Handling initially was as good as the standard MSS at moderate speeds but not satisfactory at high speeds: attributed to the increased forward weight of the engine, this was improved by fitting the heavyweight Webb girder front forks with a stiffer spring, altering the fork link lengths and lengthening the girder. To facilitate interchangeability of the QD wheels, the port-side fork end was modified to make

room for a removable spacer and a pull-out axle, as fitted to the Waycott ISDT machine.

A 6V Miller dynamo driven from the rear of the port-side crankshaft provided electrical energy for the coil ignition and lighting systems. A distributor was driven off the camshaft through an offset slot coupling to avoid mistiming during maintenance. The dynamo, voltage control unit and distributor are covered by a sheet steel enclosure at the rear of the gearbox that blends in with the fabricated rear frame section. The fuel tank is of MSS type accompanied by a two-piece seat with vestigial

View showing the stressed skin rear section.

Modification to the port-side fork end.

indications of a saddle and pillion pad. The seat is sparsely sprung so would be improved by being of one piece and more generously upholstered. The engine is located on two rubberised mounts placed on the front down tubes and one on a rear cross tube: perhaps the first instance of flexible engine mounts on a motorcycle.

The engine

It was originally intended to base the engine dimensions on MOV components of 68 x 68.5mm bore and stroke but, to test the prototype, it was decided to increase the bore to 74mm to make use of KSS pistons. This resulted in a capacity of 588cc. The aluminium barrels used in this prototype were cast in one piece with the centre lines of the bores 5.1in apart to prevent the crank webs fouling each other. It was intended to use iron barrels in production, had this materialised. The large space between the bores is used as a cooling passage, and also provides room for a central tappet block attached to the upper face of the crankcases. The barrels and heads are retained by eight long bolts that hold the whole engine in compression. The pressed-up crankshaft followed usual Veloce practice. The

Model O engine removed from the frame prior to overhaul.

webs were cut from steel plate, surface-ground parallel, and fine-bored for the mainshafts and crank pins. The hardened mainshafts were ground 3-4 thou (0.076 to 0.10m) tight. The crank pins consisted of hardened sleeves of 1.437in (36.5mm) diameter by 1.125in (28.575mm) long, lightly pressed onto 1in (25.4mm) diameter parallel steel pins that were a heavy press-fit into the crank webs.

The conrods were made from RR56 alloy and, as designed, the big and little ends were without bushes as they were intended to run directly on the crankpins and gudgeon pins. The length between centres is 5.5in (139.7mm), and both ends are 1.125in (28.575mm) wide. The aluminium crankcases are roughly cylindrical in shape; machined at both ends and on the upper and lower surfaces. The rear wall and bearing housing is integral to the cases, but the front bearing housing is attached by twelve studs to an inner strengthening wall. The crankshafts are threaded through the inner wall before the front bearing housing is fitted. All the bearings in the engine are aluminium bushes lined with white metal. The crankshafts are coupled by front-mounted gearwheels keyed to the tapered mainshafts and retained by nuts. The gear wheels have 41 straight cut teeth of 8in (203.2mm) diametrical pitch. As the crank webs were too small to provide sufficient inertia, a 7in (177.8mm) diameter cast iron flywheel was fixed to the front of the port-side crankshaft and another to the rear of the starboard crankshaft. The gears and front flywheel are enclosed by a cover, to which a pair of engine brackets are bolted to mount the engine in the frame. The contra-rotating crankshafts with 100 per cent balance factor are perfectly balanced as regards primary forces, but the secondary forces, of higher frequency, are not balanced. To prevent vibration being transmitted to the rider, the engine is rubber-mounted to provide a degree of absorption.

The timing gears and starter mechanism are mounted on the rear bearing housing driven from the port-side crankshaft. Helical cut gears, similar to those found on the M series singles, provide drive to a camshaft longitudinally-placed between the cylinders. The four cams are very close together and are of the constant acceleration type; timing was the same as the MSS, namely 60, 30, 30, 60 at 0.025in

Crankcase with kick-start driveshaft.

Cylinder bores, pistons, and tappet block.

(0.625mm) lift. The gear below the port-side crankshaft drove the gear-type oil pump and also formed part of the kick-start ratchet mechanism.

In the crankcase above the camshaft is a tappet block with hemispherical seats in the tappets for the four aluminium pushrods. The pushrods are very short.

Phil Irving was working on the design of the Model O at the same time that Willis was infatuated with the Aspin Rotary Valve. Irving was taken off Model O work to undertake testing of the Aspin head engine. Had this been successful it is probable that the O would have had Aspin valves. As it turned out, the cylinder heads are relatively conventional in design, formed in a single Y alloy casting, heavily finned with integral rocker boxes. The valve springs, guides and valve inserts are all MAC components. The Z-shaped rockers oscillate on spindles carried in posts cast on the heads, the inner ends lying in square formation in the centre, with screw adjusters at the outer ends.

Two carburettors draw fuel from a single centrally-mounted float chamber.

Oil is contained in a finned sump bolted to the crankcase, and is delivered under pressure from a gear pump to the main bearings, and from a jet to the crankshaft coupling gears. The big ends are supplied via angular holes drilled through the crankshaft webs, leading to annular recesses formed on the big end sleeves that, in turn, are slotted and drilled to convey oil to the bearing surfaces. The cams are lubricated by

Cylinder head and valves.

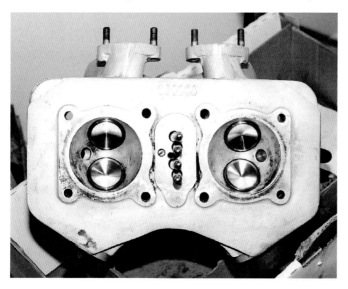

splash from the big ends. Leakage from the rear main bearings lubricates the camshaft drive, and eventually all the oil is returned to the sump.

Clutch and gearbox

The clutch is mounted on the starboard-side flywheel. Initially, it was thought that a single plate clutch would suffice, but when a change from cork inserts to the more durable Ferodo inserts was made, an additional plate was added to compensate for the low coefficient of friction of the Ferodo material. A spring loading of the order of 360lbf (1.6kN) is provided by 18 small springs similar to those used on the M series clutches. To provide a light lever operation a rack-and-pinion is installed in the upper gearbox wall. The rack pushes the upper end of a pressed steel rocking thrust plate, thereby lifting the clutch through a self-aligning ball thrust race.

Arrangement of the shafts in the gearbox was determined in part by the lubrication system of the engine. Being of the wet sump type, the engine is much taller than that of the dry sump Roarer. This has resulted in the crankshafts being at the same height as the wheel spindles to give sufficient ground clearance. As the input and output shafts are inline, it was possible to use a conventional MOV gear set but with a slightly higher 3rd gear. The input shaft runs at engine speed so the gears are required to carry a lower tooth loading than normal, and at any one moment will be transmitting power from only one cylinder, so can handle the extra power of the larger engine. The disadvantage of this arrangement, however, is that the input and output shafts are locked when 4th gear is selected, which results in the driveshaft running at engine speed. This reduces the torque transmitted by the driveshaft but also has the benefit of reducing torsional stress when the suspension moves, and allows the use of a simple universal joint. The necessary gear reduction for the rear wheel is produced by the bevel box that, by necessity, is large, and adds to the overall unsprung weight. The sleeve gear and mainshaft were redesigned to accommodate the clutch at the front and a universal joint at the rear, but there is no provision for a kick-start which operates on the port-side crankshaft. Gear selection is by the traditional selector forks

Gearbox with end cover removed, showing extension to output shaft.

Right side of gearbox.

controlled by a cam located on the offside face of the gearbox.

The kick-start on the starboard-side is external to the gearbox, and is mounted on a cross-shaft supported by a bearing on the adjacent frame lug, and in a bevel box attached to another lug on the opposite side of the frame. The output shaft from the bevel box is connected to a starting ratchet mechanism by a spring-loaded tubular coupling that allows for misalignment and is easily detachable.

The kick-start lever and foot piece can swivel in a lug splined to the cross-shaft to move them out of the way of the rider's foot, and to minimise damage in the event of a fall.

Final drive

The final drive by spiral bevel gears is in a housing bolted to the starboard fork tube, and also forms the brake backplate. The gears were supplied by David Brown and Co: two sets – one for solo and one for sidecar use. The solo ratio is 9:43 (4.77:1) and the sidecar 8:45 (5.55:1).

Use of the MOV gear train with an engine

speed clutch and driveshaft requires a larger ratio in the bevel box than that required for the Roarer. The bevel box was designed to accommodate the largest necessary crownwheel and pinion, so is slightly larger than would be required if a single ratio had been specified. The crownwheel carrier is supported on bearings in the inner wall, through which it protrudes to take the drive to the rear wheel via a splined coupling. The wheel is held in place by a removable axle located at the end of the suspension arm, and screws into a fixed steel spindle located on the outer wall of the bevel box.

The cable-operated brake shoes are carried on the bevel box and remain in place when the wheel is removed. The rear wheel can be removed by withdrawing the axle and distance piece, and moving the wheel transversely away from the bevel housing until it is clear of the brake shoes. It can then be removed rearwards, the rear bodywork being hinged to aid wheel removal. A small diameter driveshaft with a fabric universal joint at the front and a Metalistic rubber joint at the rear connects the gearbox to the bevel unit and copes with any misalignment.

On test the engine proved exceptionally

Rear suspension, bevel box, and brake shoes.

Bevel box.

smooth and vibration-free. It is inevitable that such a revolutionary design was put through a comprehensive evaluation before it could go into production. The crankshaft coupling gears did not whine but, when hot, did generate a knocking sound similar to that produced by an Ariel Square Four. Percy Goodman instigated the substitution of Tufnol gears in an attempt to quieten the engine but they disintegrated after 100 miles (160km). A cast iron set was also produced but this was no quieter than the originals.

It was whilst the cast iron set was in use that some teeth broke off, and the resulting lock-up pulled the starboard crankshaft out of line and cracked the rear crankcase wall. The crankcase was repaired and the original gears replaced. On inspection of the crankcases at the time it was discovered that the casting thickness at the crack was half the design thickness. Other changes included increasing the port-side flywheel diameter to 7.3in (185.4mm), with rim width increased to 6in (152.4mm). This increased flywheel inertia by 50 per cent, and reduced the knocking at idle to an acceptable level. The transmission and final drive are very quiet

and the engine is very flexible. Top gear can be held below 20mph (32km/hr) and the bike will accelerate smoothly to 90-95mph (144-152km/hr). The motor is vibration-free up to 6000rpm.

The lubrication system required some modification as it was felt – following a partial rear bearing seizure – that the oil was being held in the crankcases by the action of the crankshafts. To overcome this a new, longer and deeper sump was created with a sloping floor feeding the oil pump inlet. Oil pump capacity was also increased by 30 per cent. On the move the O feels like a four but without vibration: the engine cannot be felt due to the rubber mounts, and there is no sign of torque reaction. Overall it is very smooth and docile, with the flexibility that had been envisaged at its inception.

In his autobiography Phil Irving recounts a journey he made on the Model O. He set off to visit Dennis May in Kent before breakfast, a distance of 100 miles (161km). After breakfasting he rode to Bristol to have lunch with Stuart Waycott, and arrived back in Birmingham in time for tea: a total distance of around 350 miles (564km) was covered in complete comfort.

Rear wheel drive splines.

Bertie joined the Fleet Air Arm, and it seems to have been used as a factory hack until some time in the late 1940s when it was run with insufficient oil, resulting in big end failure. It was then left forlorn in the factory.

After the factory closure the Model O was acquired by John Griffith, along with the Roarer, to be displayed at Stanford Hall museum. The big ends were refurbished at this time. The Model O next passed into the care of Titch Allen in 1972, who used it to take part in the 'Ride to Europe' celebrations to mark the UK joining the common market in 1973. Unfortunately, the repair to the big end bearings was not up to the task, and the bearings needed replacing soon after by Omega Engineering, which modified the rods to accept British Leyland shells. Now part of the Rhodes Collection, the Model O has recently been the subject of an extensive overhaul, and the covers over the rear suspension units have been remanufactured.

Bertie Goodman used the machine as daily transport for two years during the war when he was an apprentice at Alfred Herbert in Coventry, finding it extremely reliable and pleasant to ride. However, on one occasion the engine suffered a broken conrod that holed the crankcase. The engine was rebuilt with strengthened conrods and the crankcase repaired.

The Model O remained in the factory when

The Model O with the 1928 TT winner at Wallington Hall, Northumberland, 2005, to celebrate the centenary of Veloce Ltd.

Table 3.2 Specifications of the Model O

Velocette 600cc Model O 1939	
Type of engine	Four-stroke twin-cylinder geared cranks OHV
Cylinders	Twin, 68 x 74mm, capacity 588cc
Compression ratio	8.4:1
Output bhp	30
Valve system	OHV, pushrod
Ignition	6 volt Miller generator, distributor with coil ignition
Engine lubrication system	Wet sump, gear oil pump
Carburettor	2 Amal type 6 bodies with common float chamber
Clutch	3-plate
Gearbox, primary and secondary drive	
Number of gears	4 MOV internals
Gearbox ratios	2.52:1, 1.75:1, 1.33:1, 1:1
Bevel box ratio (solo; sidecar)	4.77:1; 5.55:1
Overall gear ratios (solo: sidecar) : 1	12.02, 8.34, 6.34, 4.77; 13.98, 9.71, 7.38, 5.55
Final drive	Exposed driveshaft with universal joint
Frame, suspension and wheels	
Frame type	Duplex cradle with fabricated stressed skin rear section and mudguard
Front suspension	Webb girder friction-damped
Rear suspension	S/A, adjustable for load (Irving patent), Ferobestos friction bushes
Brakes, front	7in sls, internal expanding
Tyre sizes	325 x 19 front; 325 x 19 rear
Dimensions	
Wheelbase in	57
Width in	28
Height in	38
Unladen weight lb	300
Fuel tank capacity imp gall	$3^1/_2$
Oil capacity imp pt	6
Top speed mph	90-95

Model O at Wallington Hall, Northumberland.

The little engine and variations

Introduction

Throughout the history of the Veloce company, it was always the ambition of the directors to produce a motorcycle for every man: inexpensive but not cheap; easy to maintain and run. The first attempt was the belt drive Model A two-stroke of 1924 offering the sophistication of the latest two-stroke engine at an affordable price. The sidevalve model M was, perhaps, the next attempt, and spawned the MOV and the GTP.

Development of the conventional motorcycle had led to improved reliability and performance, and lessons learnt in racing resulted in the evolution of a machine that appealed to a limited market; mainly young and male. Alternative transportation methods for the vast majority of people were to walk, cycle, or, for longer distances, take the bus or train, which were not without problems. The directors of Veloce considered there was an untapped market for a trouble-free motorcycle that would cater for the transportation needs of workers, housewives

and business people in the post Second World War era. If a motorcycle was to appeal to the upwardly mobile young business person, women and professionals, features considered essential were silence, smoothness, comfort, economy, good weather protection, ease of maintenance, 20,000 miles (32,000km) between overhauls, and good quality allied to a reasonable price. It must be comfortable over any distance, and be so designed as to eliminate the need for special clothing: the rider must be shielded against road dirt, and no more than a few minutes should be required to clean the machine after the longest ride in the most inclement weather.

A preliminary design of a 150cc engine and three-speed transmission producing 5-6hp (3.75-4.5kW) at 5000rpm was undertaken by Phil Irving in 1941, when he was recovering from an injury sustained whilst fire watching at the factory. Eugene Goodman made frequent visits to Irving's home to clarify certain points, such as engine size and transmission details. The key feature of the design evolved by Irving was simplicity and ease of manufacture and maintenance. Considerations of balance and lack of vibration led to a transverse wide-angle V twin layout, with sidevalve water-cooled cylinders

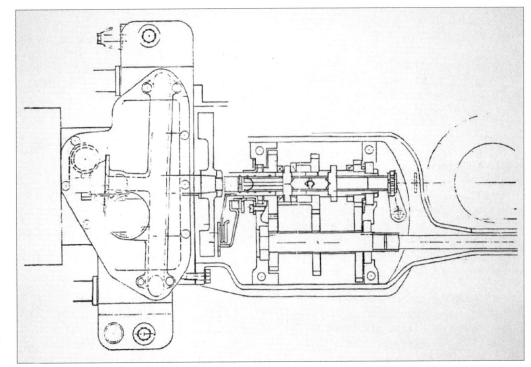

Phil Irving's three-speed gearbox with shaft drive for the LE. (Courtesy LE Owners Club)

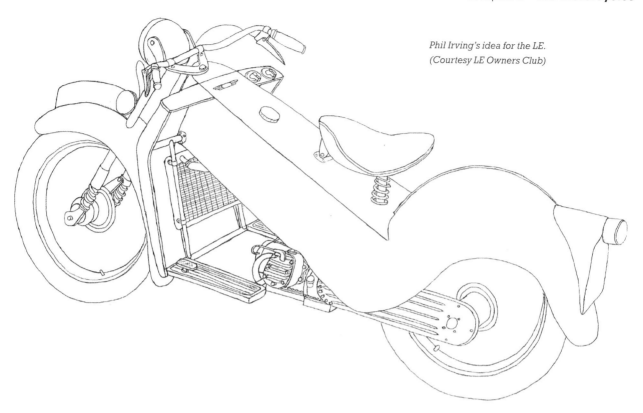

Phil Irving's idea for the LE.
(Courtesy LE Owners Club)

placed behind the rider's feet, similar to many modern scooter designs. The crankcase and cylinders were designed as one block, to which was bolted the top half of the gearbox. This assembly shared a common sump, resulting in a wet clutch and no internal oil seals. The inlet and exhaust ports were cast in the engine block, on which was fastened an alloy casting that formed the inlet tract and mounting flange for an Amal carburettor. Removal of this casting gave access to the valves and tappets, the camshaft and the crankshaft. The cylinders were water-cooled but the heads were air-cooled and could be removed without breaking a water joint.

Two quite distinct three-speed gearboxes were designed, exploring shaft or chain transmission. The shorter chain drive gearbox carried a bevel-driven cross shaft that located the final drive sprocket. The chain ran in an oil-tight cast aluminium casing strong enough to carry bending and torsional frame stresses. A spring-loaded tensioner in the cover would have kept the chain at the correct tension, and extended maintenance intervals. The cover also carried a stub axle, upon which the rear hub and brake drum were mounted for a quickly detachable rear wheel. The longer gearbox was designed for shaft drive. In both gearboxes the gear shafts were positioned side-by-side to create the offset to take the drive from the engine centre line to the driveline of the rear axle. The bearings supporting the gearbox shafts were located in housings bolted to the top of the gearbox, which allowed the gear cluster to be taken out in one piece once the bearing caps were removed.

A pressed steel frame of open U-section and wide mudguards were designed to be produced on the Lake Erie press purchased for Model O production. There was no rear suspension, but the saddle post was sprung to provide a modicum of comfort. A simple lightweight front fork was proposed, very similar to the forks fitted to the dirt track version of the K, the KDT.

Overall design was very unconventional by motorcycle standards, and in layout was very similar to a prototype R10 BMW intended for the austerity period, post-war.

Like the Model O, the Irving LE drew on practice and features more familiar to a motor car than a motorcycle, which would have resulted in low manufacturing cost, longevity and

BMW R10 prototype.

reliability. These bare bones formed the basis of a new design that was laid out by Charles Udall in 1942, coincidentally, when he was convalescing at home after an appendix operation. Having just completed the Roarer and being steeped in traditional motorcycle practice, he incorporated several of the Roarer features to produce the most sophisticated lightweight design ever conceived for a utilitarian motorcycle.

Several changes were made to the Irving design, however. Udall felt that the 150 degree twin would have given uneven firing intervals, and created problems with the design of a suitable ignition system. In addition, the resulting vibration from a V twin would have required substantial stiffening of the body structure.

Hand-built prototype LE. (Courtesy LE Owners Club)

Prototype engine with pencilled frame outline overlaid.
(Courtesy LE Owners Club)

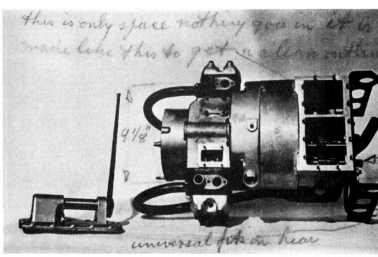

Top view of the prototype engine showing openings for tappet adjustment,
and top of the gearbox removed. Note Udall's notes on the photograph.
(Courtesy LE Owners Club)

Prototype LE at the factory, 1944. (Courtesy LE Owners Club)

THE THREE TWINS Roarer, Model O and LE

To meet the requirement of smoothness, Udall chose to use a horizontally opposed twin with the shafts located on rolling element bearings. Within a month, he had created an initial drawing and, upon approval from Eugene, set to work on detailed drawings, which took a further two months.

It is clear that the whole concept was that of an integrated design, with a primary aim to eliminate as far as possible all forms of vibration. To keep the engine as simple as practically possible, sidevalves were chosen, which also limited engine width and kept the cylinder heads within the envelope of the legshields. Shaft drive was chosen for ease of maintenance for the anticipated non-mechanically-minded rider who would appreciate reliability, and low maintenance costs as opposed to the lowest

Charles Udall on the prototype at the factory, 1944. (Courtesy LE Owners Club)

initial cost. Water cooling was chosen for two reasons: it is possible to obtain a high degree of mechanical quietness, and air cooling would have required gaps in the legshields for the cooling air stream, compromising weather protection. The manufacture of the engine, clutch, gearbox and final drive as a single unit promised simplification in assembly and build, which could not be ignored.

A hand-built prototype was created when time became available. The engine was finished in 1943 and a complete machine was ready for evaluation by 1944.

The prototype frame was largely hand-beaten, with the rear mudguard and front section produced as separate assemblies held together with six 2BA bolts. Production frames were placed in a jig and welded. In the accompanying

Prototype on test. (Courtesy LE Owners Club)

figure, the patented design of adjustable rear springing can be seen to be similar to that of the Model O.

The Mk 1 and Mk 2 models

The LE was in production for over twenty years, during which time many design modifications were incorporated. The prototypes were subjected to an extensive testing period by the works testers, who went on extended runs as far afield as Wales to test design durability. Possibly more accustomed to the traditional Velocette single, the prototypes may not have been to every tester's taste; nevertheless, they performed well under test, delivering the performance and economy expected of the design. In the hands of the public, however, shortcomings came to light, especially in the lubrication system.

During the testing period when used for extensive runs, the engines were thoroughly warmed up, but this was not typical of the use that the public made of the LE. Short trips, perhaps to the shops or to work, did not allow the engine to be completely warmed through; consequently, it tended to run cold, leading

to water condensing in the oil. This played havoc with the engine rolling element bearings, resulting in many failures and warranty claims. Clearly an unsatisfactory situation, it was resolved by replacing the rolling element bearings with squeeze film-type versions, necessitating a major redesign of the lubrication system, which occurred over several years, with modifications incorporated as they became available. As a result, several hybrid machines appeared with partly modified engines. The mains and big ends were changed by 1953, but it was not until 1955 that replacement was completed when the camshaft bearings were also modified.

Frame and cycle parts

The frame is very unconventional, being a backbone formed from 22 gauge sheet steel pressings in one piece, with a deeply valanced rear mudguard and fixing points for the rear suspension. The steering head is formed from a steel tube, machined at each end to accept the bearings, to which is wrapped around and welded a steel plate. This is pierced by four holes, such that when it is inserted into the front of the backbone, the holes line up with similar holes in the back bone. At this point the backbone is strengthened by a double skin formed by a rigid box section that also serves as a toolbox. In use, the open top of this is secured by a hinged lid. The alignment of the steering head is very important, and was achieved in assembly when the backbone and rear mudguard sections were welded together, and placed in a substantial jig, which also housed a number of compressed air actuated punches that accurately pierced all of the holes needed in the side of the body.

After painting, the box section was lined with a felt material to prevent drumming. Immediately behind the toolbox, hidden in the box section is a $1^1/_2$ gallon petrol tank mounted on brackets that also stiffen the backbone. The neck of the fuel tank protrudes through the top surface of the backbone via a rubber grommet, and is topped by a chrome-plated filler cap. To the rear of the fuel tank and underneath the sprung saddle is a well containing the battery, which is easily accessed by hinging forward the

saddle. The saddle springs are screwed into shallow cups attached to the backbone, where they are secured by being rotated through a $1/_4$ turn. To the top of the rear mudguard is welded a pressed steel platform that can be used as a luggage rack or occasional pillion seat. This is covered if a dual seat is fitted.

The 19in wheel rims are made of non-corrosive aluminium alloy, which not only reduces the unsprung weight but makes cleaning easier. The wheel hubs of nickel iron are in one piece with the brake drums, and have journal bearings separated within the hub by a hollow distance piece. Brakes are of 5in (127mm) diameter and have $^3/_4$in (19mm) wide linings. They are cable-operated and have the normal Veloce type of adjustment. Removal of the rear wheel is made possible by first removing a central spindle and distance piece, which then allows the wheel and brake to be moved forward and away from the forks, disengaging from the bevel box driving teeth and leaving the brake shoes in place on the final drive casing.

Main body, steering head and frame parts. (Courtesy LE Owners Club)

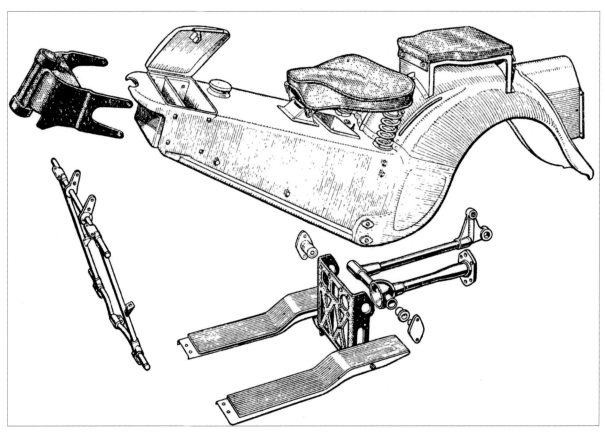

Front suspension is of the telescopic fork type: the bearing surfaces are oil-impregnated phosphor bronze bushes and each leg contains $1/8$ pint (71cc) of oil for lubrication purposes: the forks are undamped. The handlebars – formed with brackets to locate the control levers and the headlamp – are attached to the top of each fork leg by a stud that passes through the top yoke. The levers are typically Veloce, formed by folding a pressed aluminium profile: very simple but also very functional as they never snap or bend.

The rear suspension arms are attached to the swing arm unit: one on the final drive casing and the other on the opposite side leg. Being friction-damped, these are very similar to the design produced by Irving for the experimental MSS. The upper ends of the telescopic units pass through long slots in the rear mudguard and are secured by screws. This arrangement clearly follows that of the experimental MSS and Model O but is much neater in appearance. Moving the screw ends in the slots varies the effective spring rate and damping of the suspension, thus providing adjustment for varying load to give the maximum comfort for riders of any weight, and to accommodate additional loads carried in pannier bags or on the luggage rack. Attached to the rear mudguard is a fixture that houses the rear light and the number plate.

Attached to the front of the box section is a tubular frame that supports the cooling radiator and pressed aluminium legshields. The bottom member of the frame is attached to the engine unit. Instruments such as the speedometer, oil pressure gauge and switches are placed in the top of the legshields, providing a very pleasing uncluttered appearance.

The entire body, including the front forks and wheel, can be detached from the engine unit by disconnecting the rear suspension, cooling water hoses, front frame and cables, and then lifting the rear and wheeling the body forward (a modification to the front tubular frame, whereby the lower rail was attached by a serrated joint, made this operation easier).

The engine

The mechanical components of the LE were conceived to form an integrated drivetrain, similar to the Roarer, that could be assembled before connection to the body. This drivetrain comprised the engine, clutch housing, gearbox, transmission and rear suspension, plus the footboards and centre stand that are connected to the rear steady plate and radiator. This very compact unit was designed with no obvious division between the mechanical elements. Describing the engine as a separate unit is therefore somewhat artificial but it is done this way to facilitate comparison with the Roarer and Model O designs.

The engine is a horizontally opposed twin-cylinder of 150cc (later 200cc Mk 2 and Mk 3) displacement. The crankcase is of the barrel type, to which is attached on each side the cylinders and on the underside a pressed steel sump. An internal wall supports a rear bearing housing and separates the crankshaft chamber from the timing gears and reduction gear chamber. The crankshaft is threaded into the crankcase from the front and located on the rear bearing. Slots at the front face flange allow the conrods, folded into the crankshaft, to pass through the front of the crankcase to the apertures for the cylinders. The front of the crankcase is then closed by a casing that contains the front bearing housing, and also encloses the flywheel and generator set.

The crankshaft went through several evolutions during its long life. The webs and mainshafts of the two throw crankshafts are produced in one piece from 3.5 per cent nickel steel to BES69 specification. This has a high tensile strength and is ductile. Originally, the cranks were cottered to the crank pins but this was later changed to the well-tried tapered (8 thou per inch) interference fit that is a feature of Velocette engines. The Mk 1 crankshaft ran on standard ball bearings at both ends with a plain, steady bearing on the driving shaft. It was decided to use ball bearings to allow minimum resistance to starting. Two large ball bearings are sited close to the webs, a third small ball bearing is behind the flywheel, and a final plain bearing of bronze is carried in the steady plate bolted to the rear of the crankcase. In order to keep the offset on the cylinders as low as possible to reduce the out-of-balance couple to a minimum, it was desirable to minimize big end width. Thus, 28 uncaged rollers were used in the big end bearings, running on a big end track on the crankpin of 1in (25.4mm) diameter, produced from an outer sleeve of carbon-chrome steel, heat-treated and ground before being pressed on the crank pin.

Following crankshaft failures in general use due to condensation produced in the cold-running engine, which led to sludge build-up that ruined the bearings, a change was made to the journal bearings throughout. Conversion to fully plain bearings began with the Mk 2 engines, and took some time to be fully implemented, so that several hybrid engines with combinations of plane and rolling element bearings were produced. The front bearing journals are pressed onto mainshafts and located by a long circular dowel. At the rear, a single bearing journal that mates with a bronze bush in the rear wall is fixed on the mainshaft by a Woodruff key, that also locates a 21-tooth timing spur gear. The rear part of the spur gear also forms the fourth crankshaft bearing supported by the steady plate. The two bearings accommodated in the front bearing housing straddle a worm gear that drives the gear-type oil pump attached to the front bearing housing.

The four-lobe camshaft is positioned above the crankshaft, driven by a 42-tooth spur gear keyed onto the crankshaft between the two rear bearings. The camshaft is forged from case-hardened mild steel. The rear of the camshaft abuts a thrust pin located in the steady plate. The cams act on adjustable tappets that slide on very large bushes housed in the crankcase. The valves are housed in the cylinder casting, surrounded by water passages to ensure good cooling and silence in operation. Tappet adjustment is provided by an adjustable screw locked by a nut. The tappets are accessible by removing a cover plate on the crankcase, but are very difficult to adjust with the motor unit in the frame. The valve seats are machined in the cylinder castings and the guides are in cast iron pressed into the cylinder.

The little ends of the short connecting rods have wide diameter bushes to take the gudgeon pins. These are inserted into Y alloy die cast pistons with split skirts that allow very tight tolerances. Two compression rings and an oil control ring are used in each piston. The camshaft operates the sidevalves through adjustable tappets that slide in very substantial bushes. The valves of silchrome valve steel, all of which have the same head diameter, are set

at an angle in the cylinder castings, and held in their seats by single coil springs retained by the normal type of split cotter. Seat strength is 35lbf (155.6N). The valve guides are plain cast iron pressed into the cylinder casting. In the cylinder castings the water passages are designed to ensure good circulation around the valve heads, keeping them cool and silencing the noise of their operation.

It is always an issue with inline crankshafts to bring the centreline of the crankshaft into line with the transmission system. In the case of the LE, the objective is to raise the output shaft to the height of the wheel centreline, and then displace it to the left to bring it in line with the bevel box input shaft. This vertical height adjustment, and some of the sideways displacement, is achieved by the use of a helical gear pair with a reduction ratio of about 3:1 that connects the clutch to the crankshaft. This helical gear pair was lapped on a special fixture in production for quietness in operation. The smaller gear is splined to the crankshaft to the rear of the steady plate mentioned earlier. The larger gear drives a counter shaft, and is supported in a bearing on the steady plate, and by a second bearing housed in the wall of the clutch casing. The back face of this gear carries the starter ratchet mechanism, and the rearmost end of the shaft carries the clutch drive member.

Such major modifications to the bearing arrangement as have been described inevitably required substantial changes to the lubrication system. The original arrangement consisted of a gear pump housed in the lower part of the crankcase that drew oil from the sump through a gauze filter. Oil was fed from the pump to a jet that squirted lubricant onto the central web of the crankshaft. Deflectors formed on the circumference of the web led the oil onto the big end bearings. Jets also led oil to the camshaft driving gears and to the reduction gear. A further oil pipe directed oil to the plain bearing at the end of the crankshaft, and the remainder of the lubrication was by splash. Adoption of squeeze bearings that require a continuous flow of oil necessitated introduction of a maze of pipes in the sump, an oil filter, and a pressure relief pipe, the latter two items mounted externally on the right-hand side of the engine.

After passing through the oil filter the oil flows to a distribution block, where it is directed to the main bearings, the steady plate, and the rear camshaft bearing. The camshaft was made hollow to supply the front bearing and a drip feed was provided to the clutch bearing.

The carburettor

A single carburettor is used on the LE, positioned above the cylinders and connected to them by a long curving inlet tract. To ensure reliability of starting and the consistent running that it was assumed the LE owner would demand, a special carburettor was designed. At the time, no satisfactory proprietary unit was available, as the majority of engines of this size were either intended for agricultural use or as stationary engines, so could not provide the perfect tickover. Nor could they give the expected starting behaviour of enabling the engine to spring to life at the lightest pull on its starting handle.

The resulting device is the special fixed-jet carburettor designed by Udall and produced for Veloce by Amal Limited of Birmingham. The instrument is of the multi-jet type, having no needles, air or throttle slides. It contains only one moving part – a butterfly throttle – and features a separate starter jet system with in-built, push-pull operation that furnishes the correct mixture for starting and dispenses with the need for a tickler. The body has an integral float chamber and a built-in filter chamber, 4 jets and 3 spray tubes. This was difficult to set up initially as the jets were very sensitive to dirt particles; hence the need for the fuel filter. Air for the carburettor is first taken through a large air filter mounted between the two cooling elements of the radiator, then through a rubber tube to the carburettor. This arrangement reduces intake noise and also warms the inlet air for efficient vaporisation of the fuel. The inlet tract was also heated by an external tube connected to the radiator top hoses to prevent icing-up in winter.

The ignition and electrical systems

In the case of the Mk 1 LE, a BTH ignition and lighting generator unit is enclosed in a separate chamber ahead of the engine flywheel. This includes a BTH PEC DC generator, high tension coil, distributor, automatic timing device, condenser, cut-out and contact breaker. The generator is behind a pinion wheel situated on the crankshaft centreline. Below the pinion are the points and condenser, and a 6 volt coil is mounted vertically on the left. The generator cut-out is on the right at 4 o'clock. The pinion on the crankshaft meshes with a larger Bakelite distributor gear of twice the diameter, which rotates at half the crankshaft speed. The coppered spring blade that connects the coil to the centre of the Bakelite wheel forms part of the high tension circuit, as it connects to a metal distributor finger, a 'jump spark,' on the back of the distributor wheel. The two high tension contacts at 9 o'clock and 3 o'clock, which connect to the plug leads, are hidden from view. Some early Mk 1 LEs had fixed ignition timing brought about by pinning the automatic timing mechanism contained within the cam. The remaining models had automatic timing, but it is not easy to tell which is which.

With the introduction of the Mk 2 model, in 1952 the generator was changed to a 6 volt Miller AC-3 unit until engine number 200/14539. Subsequent engines were equipped with the AC-3P, which was then replaced by the AC-4 unit in 1953 from engine number 200/29253. The AC-4 unit was used on the Mk 3 model until engine number 6533/3 of 1964, when a 12V Lucas unit was adopted.

The Miller generator combines coil ignition with two 6 volt coils wired in series, thus providing an idle spark for each cylinder with a flywheel generator. An automatic advance and retard mechanism, using the more conventional bob weight system, is placed on the front end of the crankshaft. The flywheel magnets energise three low tension lighting coils fixed to the flywheel side of the stator plate. The whole unit is very compact and fits in the space previously occupied by the BTH generator. It is enclosed by a large pan-like cover fixed on long studs located in the stator plate. The AC current generated is rectified by a disc rectifier bolted underneath the fuel tank. When the ignition switch is live only one of the three lighting coils is in circuit to supply the two high tension ignition coils and provide a small charging current. When lights are required, all three

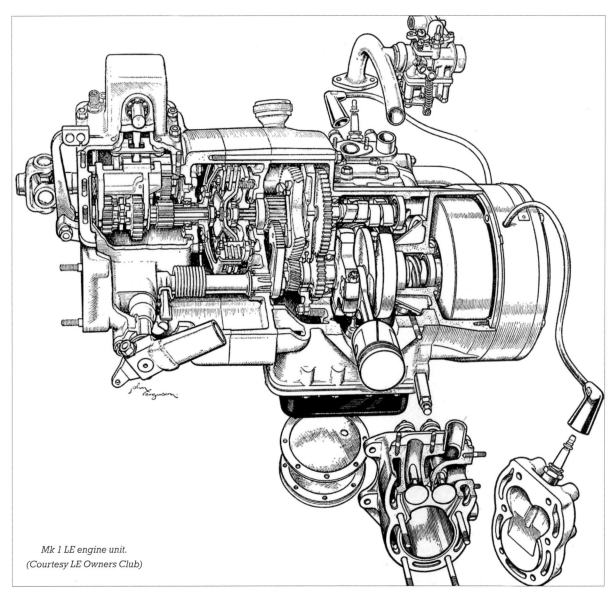

Mk 1 LE engine unit.
(Courtesy LE Owners Club)

coils are connected into the circuit to supply the higher charge necessary. The generator is designed so that the output exactly matches the load at an engine speed equivalent to 25mph (40km/hr) in top gear. No form of regulation is thus required. The AC-3P generator is equipped with a safety cut-out that prevents damage if the battery, which is housed under the saddle, is wired incorrectly.

The electrical controls are mounted on top of the right-hand legshield. Early models had two switches, with a red warning light between them:

the right-hand switch for the ignition and the left-hand for the lights. When the ignition switch is turned to the right, the red light glows to indicate current flow through the coil, and goes out when the engine has reached a suitable speed. An emergency starting facility is provided in the eventuality of a flat battery: the switch is turned to the left and the engine can be started and run at low speeds without the battery. Later models have, at the top of the right legshield, one switch with a central key; to its left an ammeter. In this case there is no warning light.

Clutch and gearbox

The clutch is very unconventional by Veloce standards, with three friction plates (two on the Mk 1) and eight springs to clamp it all together. It consists of a circular backplate that is attached to the reduction gear shaft by splines and a locknut. eight long studs are located on this in equally spaced holes on a 5-inch pitch circle, and secured by a lock nut. Between these studs are eight more equally-spaced holes, into which are placed thimble-like spring cups. A pressure plate is passed over the studs above the springs, alternately followed by tongued friction plates (to engage with the clutch bell) and driving plates that are threaded over the studs. The whole assembly is compressed against the springs by nuts that are run down the threaded end of the eight studs.

The clutch, which is a close copy of that found on the Roarer, is operated through a lever pivoted at the back of the gearbox, and bearing against a rod that passes through the hollow mainshaft to apply pressure to the pressure plate to compress the clutch springs. The clutch friction plates are of Ferodo UM41 high fade-point material. To reduce spring pressure three friction plates (two on the Mk 1) are used to transmit power. The clutch bell is splined onto the gearbox input shaft. The clutch is situated in a separate dry chamber between the crankcase and the gearbox, formed by a housing that is part of the gearbox. In total, four pieces of casing are joined together by studs and dowels to form one compact assembly very similar to the Roarer. The reduction gear reduces the speed of the clutch, increasing the torque transmitted into the gearbox but making the gearchange smoother, and reversing the direction of rotation of the clutch relative to the flywheel. The advantages of contra-rotating masses illustrated in the Roarer and Model O have been applied to the LE also. The starting mechanism consists of a starter gear on the counter shaft that is connected to the back of the reduction gear by spring pawls. Turning the starter gear through the hand-operated mechanism rotates the reduction gear and hence the engine. The additional benefit of the reduction gear can be seen as a 90 degree movement of the starter handle provides 270 degrees of crankshaft movement; more than enough to start a twin. The mechanism is clever because, as the starter gear is on the engine side of the clutch, in the event of a stall in traffic, the engine can be restarted with the clutch disengaged, negating the need to find neutral in the gearbox.

The three-speed all-indirect constant mesh gearbox is of the crossover type; the shafts side-by-side to obtain the required lateral displacement of the driveline. The gear shafts are produced in a Ni-Cr case hardening steel EM39, and the gears are made of the same material as the reduction gear for the same reasons. The gearbox is very similar in concept to that of the Roarer, inasmuch as the drive is taken in on one shaft and the output taken from the other: in other words, it's not a straight-through box, and the drive is always transmitted by one pair of gears only in any gear.

The input and output shafts are carried on ball bearings located in the casing at the rear, and in a bearing plate at the front, and carry three pairs of gear wheels which are in constant mesh. A single row of dogs – part of the input shaft – drive either the second- or third-speed pinions. A selector formed as a bridge locates the two free-running gears each side of the dogs, and moves them axially on the shaft as a pair to engage one with the dogs. The sliding wheels are not splined to the shaft but are free to rotate on them when not transmitting power. The matching pinions are splined on the output shaft, and, as they are formed as a double gear, require a single selector fork to move them along the shaft. The front free face of this double gear has dogs that can engage with the first gear pinion at the front end of the output shaft. The first gear pinion, when the dogs are disengaged, is free to rotate on the output shaft, and is driven by its matching pinion that is splined to the input shaft.

Gear changing in the Mk 1 and Mk 2 is carried out through the movement of normal selectors, operated by a hand lever on the offside of the machine working through a car-type gate that passes through neutral at each gearchange. The starting mechanism is a hand lever mounted on the offside of the gearbox, as described earlier. As the starting handle is gently pulled rearward, it automatically raises the centre stand should it be in the down position.

This choice of hand starter and gearchange was considered very early in drawing up the specification of the machine, bearing in mind

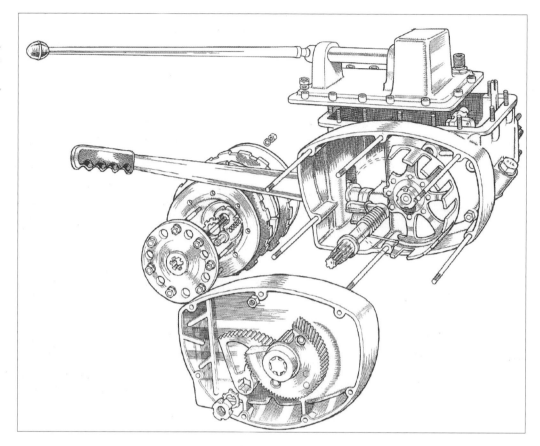

Clutch housing, reduction gear and hand-start mechanism. (Courtesy LE Owners Club)

the importance of attracting a new type of motorcyclist. This arrangement negated the risk of damage to shoes, ankles and clothing; the effort required could be exerted by a child, and the inter-coupling of the stand with the starter ensured there was no danger of moving off without the stand being lifted. The centre stand is pivoted on a steel pressing of shallow section, liberally pierced with holes, that is fastened to the rear face of the gearbox. This is the rear frame crossmember, where the swing arm assembly and back brake pedal are located, as well as the lower support for the body.

Final drive

The rear suspension and final drive clearly draw on the design developed by Udall for the Roarer, but modified to aid assembly and reduce cost (to a certain extent). The rear fork pivots on hard chromium-plated pins attached to a flange

that is bolted to the frame crossmember. The pins bear on oil-impregnated phosphor bronze bushes set into the swing arm. This is in contrast to the Roarer, where the pins were part of the swing arm, and is a much better arrangement for ease of assembly. The original swing arm was a steel fabrication very similar to that fitted to the Roarer, but was changed to a neater aluminium casting. The driveshaft produced from a Ni-Cr oil-hardened steel of 65 tons tensile strength is enclosed within the left-hand fork tube, which has a large bell at the front to accommodate a universal joint and a felt seal. The pivot of the suspension is on the centreline of the UJ to minimise distortion through movement of the suspension.

The rear face has a flange, to which is located the bevel box. This houses a spiral bevel pinion and crown wheel manufactured from 3 per cent Ni-Cr-Moly steel of 70-80 tons tensile strength, which is tough with a high core strength. This assembly is much smaller than that on the Model O due to the effect of the reduction gear. The bevel box casing comprises a cover located by dowels onto the left-hand face of the bevel drive casing. A fixed spindle runs through the bevel box casing, and is secured to the cover by a key, washer and locknut. This is placed in the centre of the crown wheel assembly, which runs on bearings set in the cover and the casing, and protrudes through to the right-hand side of the casing. This side of the casing forms the brake plate to which the brake shoes are attached and activated by a cable-operated cam located in the casing. The brake drum is one piece with the wheel hub, which has a gear ring machined on a central boss to engage with a male form of the teeth machined into the end of the bevel gear shaft. The wheel hub is slid into place and retained by a spindle that passes through the right-hand side fork leg end, through a distance piece, and is then screwed into the blind end of the fixed spindle. The entire assembly is very neat and requires no adjustment: clearly, wheel alignment will not be lost if the rear wheel is removed.

The twist grip is as unconventional as many of the LE's features. Situated on the right-hand handlebar, as the grip is twisted, a small brass block within is made to travel down a quick spiral. The throttle wire is attached to this block, so receives a straight pull, which reduces fraying and breakage that tends to happen when the wire is twisted. The block and spiral are contained in two close-fitting brass tubes, factory-assembled with grease that should last the lifetime of the machine. The effort required to turn the grip is regulated by releasing a dome nut at the end of the grip, adjusting a set screw that alters the pressure between the two sleeves, and then tightening the dome nut.

The LE's design sophistication came with a price: performance and styling did not appeal to experienced motorcyclists, and the retention of traditional motorcycle design did not attract new customers (particularly women, who would have preferred an open frame). The LE has been compared to an Austin 7 with a Rolls-Royce price tag. This combination of superb specification and Veloce's obsession with fine engineering made competitive pricing with other manufacturers somewhat difficult to achieve: the Mk 1 sold at £126.00 against the BSA D1 Bantam at £76.00. The LE was, in effect, a

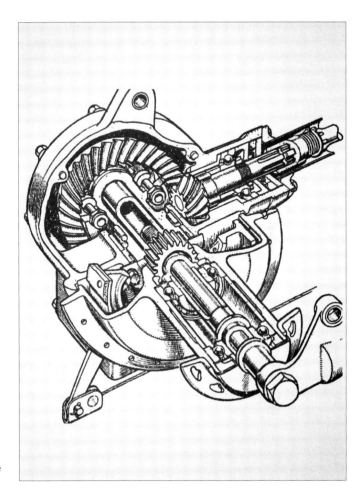

Bevel box with rear brake, wheel hub and distance piece.

two-wheeled car, yet the full-sized wheels, the excellent rigid chassis, and the exceptionally low centre of gravity meant that none of the motorcycle's virtues had been skimped on.

Titch Allen, the famous columnist, described the LE as: "an economy lightweight which ended up as the most sophisticated pure design in motorcycle history." Projected sales of 300 per week were never achieved over the production life of the model, and failure of the LE to penetrate the mass market is considered by many to have led to the eventual demise of the company: perhaps unjustified when competitor machines available at the time of the launch of the LE are considered. Many were powered by proprietary two-stroke engines of dubious reliability, not attractive to the type of client Veloce was trying to entice to motorcycling.

This is shown in the accompanying

table3.3 taken from period road tests, which indicates that the LE could hold its own with its competitors in performance and fuel consumption, but was considerably more expensive. Twenty years later, of course, the LE was beginning to show its age, and could not compete with products from the Japanese manufacturers.

Layout of the controls from the Owners Handbook.

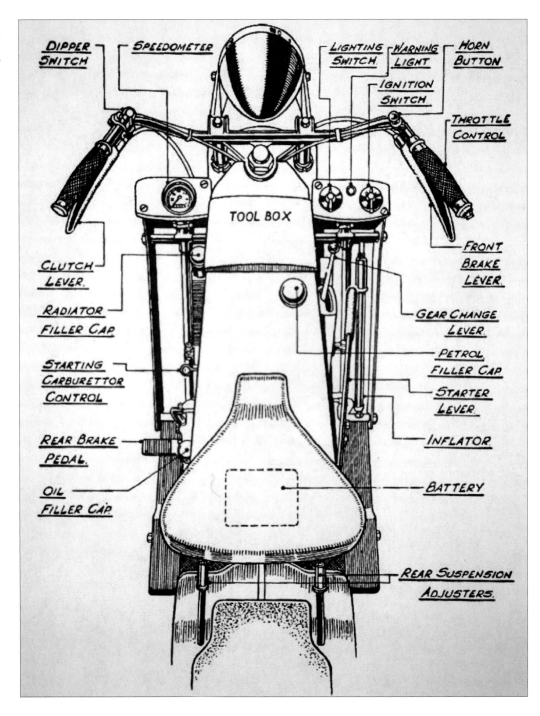

Table 3.3 The LE's competitors

Make, 2- or 4-stroke, side (sv) or overhead (ohv) valve	Year	Model	Capacity cc, no of cylinders	Top speed (mph)	Fuel consumption at 30, 40, 50mph	Weight (lb)	Price new (£.s.d)
BSA, 4, sv	1951	C11	249, 1	64	118, 94, 82	309	£142.4.10
BSA, 4, ohv	1953	C10	249, 1	56	120, 92, 76	318	£129.5.10
BSA, 2	1954	Bantam	148, 1	53	150, 128, 104	217	£82.0.0
BSA, 2	1959	Bantam	123, 1	46	144, 112, NA	171	£74.3.6
Brockhouse, 4, sv	1954	Indian Brave	248, 1	58	117, 87, 76	279	£115.15.0
Bown, 2, Villiers	1952	Tourist	122, 1	45	128, 80, NA	172	£103.0.0
DMW, 2, Villiers 10D	1953	Lightweight	122, 1	47	120, 90, NA	158	£93.12.6
DMW, 2, Villiers 1H	1954	Cortina	197, 1	58	112, 101, 88	197	£131.12.3
DOT, 2, Villiers	1949	RS	197, 1	54	144, 120, 104	229	£106. 17.6
Excelsior, 2	1952	Talisman	172, 2	64	96, 88, 67	250	173.15.7
Francis Barnett, 2, AMC	1959	Cruiser	172, 1	57	120, 106, 95	245	£164.13.5
Greeves, 2, Villiers	1953	20D	197, 1	57	112, 90, 68	215	£150.0.0
James, 2, Villiers	1950	Captain	197, 1	56	110, 102, 92	215	£111.2.6
James, 2, Villiers	1951	Commodore	98, 1	39	172, 144, NA	161	£66.4.0
James, 2, Villiers	1953	Cadet	122, 1	46	128, 100, NA	168	£84.11.8
Norman, 2, Villiers	1953	Springer B2S	197, 1	60	110, 96, 64	244	£138.9.7
Tandon, 2, Villiers	1951	Supaglide	197, 1	55	98, 80, NA	184	£125.1.11
Velocette, 4, sv	**1951**	**LE II**	**192, 2**	**57**	**119, 108, 100**	**268**	**£168.18.3**

Table 3.4 Mk 1 LE specifications

Velocette 150 cc model Mk 1 LE 1948-1950	
Type of engine	Four-stroke water-cooled SV
Cylinders	Twin, 44 x 49mm, capacity 149cc
Compression ratio	6:1
Output bhp	6 @ 5000rpm
Valve system	Sidevalve
Generator and ignition	6 volt BTH 30W dynamo, 10mm sparkplugs, coil ignition
Engine lubrication system	Wet sump, gear oil pump in sump, spray and splash
Carburettor	Veloce multi-jet
Clutch	2-plate Veloce
Gearbox, primary and secondary drive	
Reduction gear ratio	3.27:1
Number of gears	3
Gearbox ratios	2.078:1, 1.105:1, 0.739:1
Bevel box final drive ratio	3:1
Overall gear ratios	20.4:1, 10.85:1, 7.256:1
Final drive	Enclosed shaft in swing arm with UJ at rear suspension pivot
Frame, suspension and wheels	
Frame type	Pressed steel box section with integral rear mudguard
Front suspension	Friction damped telescopic
Rear suspension	S/A adjustable Irving patent, friction damped spring units
Brakes: front, diameter, width in	5 x 0.75 (to 1954), 5 x 1
Brakes: rear, diameter, width, in	5 x 0.75 (to 1954), 5 x 1
Rim sizes	WM1 x 19 f, WM1 x 19 r to 1956, then WM2
Tyre sizes	3.00 x 19 f, 3.00 x 19 r to 1956, then 3.25 x 18

(continues overleaf)

Velocette 150 cc model Mk 1 LE 1948-1950	
Dimensions	
Overall length, wheelbase in	82, 51.2
Width in	25
Seat height in	28
Unladen weight lb	250
Fuel tank capacity imp gall	1.25
Oil capacity imp pt	1.25
Gearbox capacity imp pt	0.25
Standard fuel consumption mpg	90-100
Top speed mph	50mph
Frame number	Stamped on plate attached to underside of toolbox lid
Engine number	Stamped on crankcase, below carburettor

Table 3.5 Mk 2 LE specifications

Velocette 200cc Mk 2 LE 1950-1958	
Type of engine	Four-stroke water-cooled SV
Cylinders	Twin, 50 x 49mm capacity 192cc
Compression ratio	6:1/7:1
Output bhp	8 @ 5000rpm
Valve system	Sidevalve
Generator and ignition	6 volt BTH 30W dynamo to 1951, then 6 volt Miller 42W alternator for some 10mm sparkplugs, coil ignition
Engine lubrication system	Wet oil in sump, squeeze film bearings
Carburettor	Veloce multi-jet
Clutch	2-plate, 3-plate from 05/1953
Gearbox, primary and secondary drive	
Reduction ratio	3.27:1
Number of gears	3
Gearbox ratios	2.14:1, 1.325:1, 0.728:1
Bevel box final drive ratio	3:1
Overall gear ratios	21:1, 13:1, 7.15:1
Final drive	Enclosed shaft in swing arm with UJ at rear suspension pivot
Frame, suspension and wheels	
Frame type	Pressed steel box section with integral rear mudguard
Front suspension	Friction damped telescopic
Rear suspension	S/A adjustable Irving patent, friction damped spring units
Brakes front, diameter, width in	5 x 0.75; 5 x 1.0 from 05/1953
Brakes rear, diameter, width, ins	5 x 0.75, 5 x 1.0 from 05.1953
Rim sizes	WM1-LA x 19 f, WM1-LA x 19 r, WM2 from 1956
Tyre sizes	3.00 x 19 f, 3.00 x 19 r, 300 x 18 f, 300 x 18 r from 1956
Dimensions	
Overall length, wheelbase in	82, 51.2
Width in	25
Seat height in	28
Unladen weight lb	250
Fuel tank capacity imp gall	1.25, 1.62 from 05/1953
Oil capacity imp pt	1.25, 1.75 from 05/1953
Gearbox capacity imp pt	0.25
Standard fuel consumption	90 to 100
Top speed mph	52 to 55
Frame number	Stamped on plate attached to underside of toolbox lid
Engine number	Stamped on crankcase below carburettor

The Valiant and Mk 3 LE

Veloce surprised everyone at the 1956 motorcycle show when it unveiled the air-cooled Valiant in an attempt to compete in the market for sports machines of under 250cc. The engine and transmission was based on the LE but, in this case, the cylinders were air-cooled and the overhead valves were operated by pushrods. A new design of loop cradle frame was developed that gave very good handling. Perhaps this was an attempt by Veloce to improve sales of the flat twin and recover some of the tooling costs expended on the LE?

The design was executed by Charles Udall, who was inevitably compromised by the requirement to use as many of the original LE tools, jigs and fixtures as possible in order to reduce production costs.

The revised engine had an increased compression ratio of 8.5: 1 and an anticipated output of 12hp, which necessitated widening the big end bearings and lengthening the crankcase to accommodate a wider central crankshaft web. The changes were also incorporated into a revised LE, which became known as the Mk 3 LE.

The frame and cycle parts

A new duplex cradle frame was designed for the Valiant, which, in terms of geometry, owes a lot to the Roarer frame with twin down tubes, a large diameter backbone, and widely splayed tubes at the rear in place of the usual seat post. Of all-welded construction, the frame was produced by Reynolds Tubes. Unlike the Roarer, however, the lower frame rails are part of the frame, with no attempt made to split the engine and drive unit from the upper frame elements. The rear frame crossmember of the LE gave way to two smaller brackets located on the gearbox rear face, which locate the swing arm pivots and also form the rear attachments to the frame. The footrests, rear brake and centre stand are located on attachments to the lower frame tubes. Apart from this there is no reason to provide the lower frame tubes as the engine and gearbox units could have been a stressed member, as in the LE.

The frame is heavily gusseted around the head stock and the subframe is welded to the main structure. The front suspension uses LE forks that carry a sports mudguard supported by a cross stay on each side, and Woodhead-Munroe spring damper units control the rear suspension. LE wheels are used with full width hubs and single leading shoe brakes of 5in diameter and 1in width. The rear mudguard is slightly valanced and is supported on stays at the rear that also serve as lifting handles.

A three-gallon petrol tank mounted on rubbers is held in place by a quick-release centre strap located at the rear by a hook on the frame, and at the front on pins set each side of the head stock. A toolbox to house the battery, fitted to the offside of the frame, could be matched by another on the nearside. This additional toolbox and engine crash bars were optional extras, as were pillion footrests.

The handlebars bolted to the top of the front forks are tidied up with a fork shroud and headlamp housing. The headlamp shell housed the main lighting and ignition switch; the speedometer in the centre and an ammeter on the offside to balance the lighting switch. A novel feature at the time was a pressed steel cover that enclosed the upper parts of the engine and gearbox. This was pressed in two parts and held together by screws. A circular aperture at the front provided a location for the horn that was mounted in a rubber ring sandwiched between the two halves of the cowl.

The engine

The Valiant engine and running gear draw heavily on the LE, but significant changes were made to cope with the increased power output and to give the machine a sporting appearance. To this effect, the final design incorporated an air-cooled OHV engine with a four-speed, foot-operated gearbox coupled to the LE final drive. To cope with the extra power output the crankshaft, of the same constructional details as the LE, was stiffened with wider webs ($1/2$ inch (12.2mm) thickness), and the big ends were widened to become 0.4in (10mm). The main bearings were also lengthened slightly. The big ends were split shells pressed into the eyes of the steel connecting rods and the little ends were bushed. These modifications and the lengthened crankcase also became standard components of the Mk 3 LE. The shallow dome

Nearside view of a Valiant.

Three-quarter view of a Valiant.

pistons had cutaways in the crown for the two valves, and had one scraper ring and two compression rings.

The cylinders were cast in iron and included aluminium pushrod tubes that were an interference fit in the top and bottom flanges. The cylinder heads were cast in light alloy with shrunk-in-place valve seats. A camshaft, giving a greater lift and dwell than that of the LE, operated tappets and pushrods that actuated rockers in the cylinder head. The rockers were mounted on cast-in pillars in the head and pivoted on eccentric pins (as with the Mk 7 and Mk 8 KTTs and the Mk 2 KSS) that were rotated to set valve clearance. The rocker box was enclosed by a cast aluminium domed cover pulled down by two screws.

The lubrication system was entirely LE, complemented by an external pipe that fed the rockers from the top of the timing chest. On the face of it, it seems strange that Veloce should have persisted with the journal bearing arrangement for the Valiant as, being air-cooled, it could be expected that this engine would run hotter and not suffer from the Mk 1 LE's oil sludge problems. Also, rolling element bearings are more forgiving with regard to oil supply, so it's likely the reliability problems that subsequently beset the Valiant could have been avoided.

The front of the engine carried the same Miller generator as the LE, but the advance and retard unit gave a different advance curve to suit the OHV engine.

When first envisaged, a single carburettor

mounted centrally above the crankcase was considered. This required a long length of induction pipe which would have given a throttle response scarcely quick enough for a sporting bike. The potential throttle response problem was overcome by using an Amal 363 carburettor with built-in wire gauze strangler attached to a short stub intake manifold on each cylinder. The exhaust pipes were very straightforward, with each cylinder having a long exhaust pipe that ran back under the cylinder barrel to a torpedo-type silencer attached to the rear subframe.

Clutch and gearbox

The Valiant's clutch is essentially that of the LE, with three driven plates and bonded Ferodo friction rings. The starter mechanism incorporates a kick-start that required modification to the LE starter quadrant.

The movement of the lever is rather short, and restricted by a rubber stop to prevent it going too far and disengaging the internal mechanism. A four-speed gear cluster was devised, compact enough to fit into the LE

The Valiant engine in section.

SECTION THROUGH PORTS

ECCENTRIC PIN ADJUSTMENT

gearbox, which was changed slightly to have only four mounting points on the rear face, and for the speedometer drive to be located at the front left corner, driven by a worm gear on the output shaft. Input and output shafts are carried on ball bearings located in the casing at the rear and in a bearing plate at the front. As with the three-speed design, a single row of dogs on the input shaft drive either the third or fourth speed pinion. A selector formed as a bridge locates the two free-running gears each side of the dogs, and moves them axially on the shaft as a pair to engage with the dogs. The matching pinions are splined on the output shaft and, as they are formed as one piece, require a single selector fork to move them along the shaft. The free ends of this double gear have dogs that can engage with gears at each end of the output shaft to provide first and second gears. The first and second gear pinions are free to rotate on the output shaft, and are driven by matching pinions splined to the input shaft.

The selector forks slide on rods located in the top of the gearbox, and are positioned by a selector face cam pivoted in the gearbox top cover. Above the selector cam is the positive stop mechanism that is moved by a horizontal shaft set across the cover. The shaft extends to the outside of the gearbox where an external leaver connects it via a rod link to the foot change lever. The remainder of the transmission is as the LE. Clearly, Charles Udall drew on the Roarer's gearbox arrangement in designing the four-speed gearbox for the Valiant.

With the 250cc class popular in the UK, few enthusiasts were interested in an expensive 200cc motorcycle, especially one with a four-stroke flat-twin instead of the more familiar four-stroke single or two-stroke twin. Sales of the Valiant were sluggish and not helped when new regulations that limited learner capacity to 250cc persuaded other manufacturers to produce models of this capacity.

Veloce really had made a bad call. If the Valiant could have been enlarged to 250cc it may have sold in large numbers, but adoption of many LE parts prevented this. The main obstacle lay with the proximity of the camshaft to the crankshaft, and the large big end eyes that prevented the stroke being enlarged as these parts would have come into contact.

The decision to continue with the squeeze film bearings from the LE is curious, given that an air-cooled engine would run hotter, and would likely not suffer from the LE's condensation problems.

It is also curious that, at this time, the

company was developing an industrial engine based on the LE that reverted to the rolling element bearings of the initial design. Had this been done in the case of the Valiant it would have been possible to use a conrod with a smaller big end eye, as with modern two-stroke engines, allowing the stroke to be enlarged to produce an engine of 250cc capacity.

1600 Valiants were made between 1957 and 1963, so it is a relatively rare motorcycle today. Several Valiants have been resurrected by using LE engines, which has improved reliability.

Table 3.6 Valiant specifications

Velocette 200cc Valiant 1956-1964	
Type of engine	Four-stroke air-cooled OHV
Cylinders	Twin, 50 x 49mm capacity 192cc
Compression ratio	8.5:1
Output bhp	12 @ 6000rpm; 7000 from 1958
Valve system	OHV, pushrod, rockers on eccentric spindles
Generator and ignition	6 volt Miller 42W alternator, 10mm sparkplugs, coil ignition
Engine lubrication system	Wet sump, gear oil pump in sump, squeeze film bearings
Carburettor	2 Amal 363/4 or 363/5
Clutch	3-plate Veloce
Gearbox, primary and secondary drive	
Reduction gear ratio	3.27:1
Number of gears	3
Gearbox ratios	2.078:1, 1.353:1, 1.0:1, 0.739:1
Bevel box final drive ratio	3:1
Overall gear ratios	20.4:1, 13.28:1, 9.818:1, 7.256: 1
Final drive	Enclosed shaft in swing arm with UJ at rear suspension pivot
Frame, suspension and wheels	
Frame type	Welded tube
Front suspension	Friction damped telescopic
Rear suspension	S/A non-adjustable
Brakes, front, diameter, width in	5 x 1.0
Brakes, rear, diameter, width, in	5 x 1.0
Rim sizes	WM2 x 18 f, WM2 x 18 r
Tyre sizes	3.25 x 18 f, 3.25 x 18 r
Dimensions	
Overall length, wheelbase in	82in, 51.2
Width in	25
Seat height in	28
Unladen weight lb	255
Fuel tank capacity imp gall	3.0
Oil capacity imp pt	1.75
Gearbox capacity imp pt	0.25
Standard fuel consumption mpg	90 to 100
Top speed mph	67
Frame number	Stamped on left-hand side rear suspension bracket
Engine number	Initially stamped on crankcase below carburettor; later on right-hand side of crankcase ahead of cylinder barrel

The Mk 3 LE

The Mk 3 LE engine is essentially a water-cooled sidevalve version of the Valiant engine and transmission unit, housed in the LE frame and cycle parts. Many of the interesting and unique features that made the LE such an integrated design were dispensed with, as proprietary components were substituted for the special in-house items. An Amal 363 carburettor replaced the multi-jet, and the very efficient inlet filter, heater and silencing arrangement was dispensed with. A conventional Amal throttle was substituted for the straight pull Veloce design.

In adopting the kick-start and foot gearchange of the Valiant, Veloce must have realised that the perceived market for the LE – non-conventional motorcyclists, housewives and office workers – no longer existed, so it modified the design to suit its biggest customer, the UK constabulary. Changes were also made to the cycle parts, the speedometer was now housed in the head lamp shell, and the position of the ignition switch and ammeter seem to have been determined by which design of shell was available on assembly, as some retained these items in the top of the legshields and in others they were in the headlamp shell.

Table 3.7 Mk 3 LE specifications

Velocette 200 cc Mk 3 LE 1958-1971	
Type of engine	Four-stroke water-cooled SV
Cylinders	Twin, 50 x 49mm, capacity 192cc
Compression ratio	7:1
Output bhp	8 @ 5000rpm
Valve system	Sidevalve
Generator and ignition	6 volt Miller 42W alternator or 80W, 12 volt Lucas 90W alternator from 1965, 10mm sparkplugs, coil ignition
Engine lubrication system	Wet sump, gear oil pump in sump, spray and splash
Carburettor	Amal 363
Clutch	3-plate Veloce
Gearbox, primary and secondary drive	
Reduction gear ratio	3.27:1
Number of gears	4
Gearbox ratios	2.078:1, 1.353:1, 1.0:1 0.739:1
Bevel box final drive ratio	3:1
Overall gear ratios	20.4:1, 13.28:1, 9.818:1, 7.256:1
Final drive	Enclosed shaft in swing arm with UJ at rear suspension pivot
Frame, suspension and wheels	
Frame type	Pressed steel box section with integral rear mudguard
Front suspension	Friction damped telescopic
Rear suspension	S/A adjustable Irving patent, friction damped spring units
Brakes, front, diameter, width in	5 x 1
Brakes, rear, diameter, width, in	5 x 1
Rim sizes	WM2 x 18 f, WM2 x 18 r
Tyre sizes	3.25 x 18 f, 3.25 x 18 r
Dimensions	
Overall length, wheelbase in	82, 51.2
Width in	25
Seat height in	28
Unladen weight lb	263
Fuel tank capacity imp gall	1.62
Oil capacity imp pt	1.75
Gearbox capacity imp pt	0.25
Standard fuel consumption mpg.	90 to 100
Top speed mph	50 to 55 at 5000rpm
Frame number	Stamped on plate attached to underside of toolbox lid
Engine number	Stamped on crankcase, below carburettor

The hole in the body for the gearchange lever was no longer required. The front forks were tided up and, by using the Valiant headlamp shrouds, looked more modern: wheel hubs became full width, although the brake shoes remained 1 inch wide. The legshields now carried the horn on the offside, and the licence holder was sited on the nearside, having moved from the front number plate.

A range of optional extras was made available, including some stylish panniers, a dual seat, a windscreen and an auxiliary fuel tank. The LE then tended to become a rather unusual-looking conventional motorcycle, but without the endearing features or build quality of the Mk 1 and Mk 2.

The extra power available from the strengthened crankshaft and the four-speed gearbox improved performance, making the Mk 3 a delight to ride, especially for the more mature rider. Brisk riding could be achieved in traffic, with 40mph (64km/hr) available in second gear and 50mph (80km/hr) in third.

The civilian market was diminishing as the styling did not appeal to younger riders more interested in the sporty look of the Royal Enfield GT and the Honda Benley. The LE remained very popular with police forces, however, as it was an ideal vehicle for quickly and quietly transporting constables around their beat: subsequent design changes were intended to improve performance for this activity.

In 1965 the electrics were changed to 12 volt using Lucas parts. A Zenor diode was placed under the toolbox and battery capacity was increased. Within the engine the timing gears were enlarged in width, and oil feed into the crankshaft increased. The cylinder castings were modified to enlarge the cylinder head gasket area. The propeller shaft was waisted to improve drive flexibility, and the crown wheel and pinion were strengthened. An Amal type 19 carburettor was adopted and the main frame pressing was strengthened by using thicker gauge steel.

The final modification occurred in 1967 when stiffening was added to the underside of the body. From then on the LE continued unchanged.

8070 Mk 3s were produced between 1958 and close of production in 1971, the majority of sales going to the constabulary.

In total, some 30,000 LEs of all marks were produced, equivalent to half the total number of motorcycles produced by Veloce over the company's lifetime.

The Vogue

In an attempt to provide a deluxe version of the LE, the Vogue was presented to the public at the 1962 Motorcycle Show. The power and transmission unit was identical to that of the Mk 3 LE, and other common parts included forks and wheels. The frame was quite different to the LE, however, being fabricated with a single backbone and rear subframe with brackets that located on the rear frame crossmember, and a frame tube assembly at the front that located on the radiator. Frame production was poor by Veloce standards, with no concern for aesthetics or quality of finish: out of sight, out of mind may well have been the dictum in this case.

The rear, non-adjustable suspension units attached to the rear subframe. Minor changes were made to some of the components to make way for the close-fitting body. The external oil filter was moved from the right-hand side cylinder head to attach to the crankcases mounted on the bolts locating the reduction gear steady plate. The front frame tube assembly was also slightly narrower at the bottom to accommodate the legshields.

Meant to appeal to 'Mr Everyman,' the Vogue was supposed to be a luxurious step up from basic transport. Fully enclosed in fibreglass bodywork, with windscreen, legshields, and – later – panniers, it addressed a big problem for British riders: riding in the rain. Twin headlamps and flashing indicators made the Vogue a very distinctive and practical machine, and its bodywork helped shield the rider and made the machine much easier to keep clean. With all of the bodywork and additional accoutrements the Vogue was heavy, but a delight to ride with all-day cruising around 50mph very possible. A beautiful piece of work, finely-crafted fibreglass panels fit nicely together to make a lovely, yet functional shape. Engine access was via removable panels located with Dzus fasteners. Despite this, however, it seems that Veloce misread the market: the Vogue never became popular and went out of production in 1968, after a run of just 371 machines.

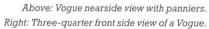
Above: Vogue nearside view with panniers.
Right: Three-quarter front side view of a Vogue.

Table 3.8 Vogue specifications

Velocette 200cc Vogue 1963-1968	
Type of engine	Four-stroke water-cooled SV
Cylinders	Twin, 50 x 49mm, capacity 192cc
Compression ratio	7:1
Output bhp	8 @ 5000rpm
Valve system	Sidevalve
Generator and ignition	6 volt Miller 42 or 80W alternator, 12 volt Lucas alternator from 1965, 10mm sparkplugs, coil ignition
Engine lubrication system	Wet sump, gear oil pump in sump, squeeze film bearings
Carburettor	Amal 363 or type 19
Clutch	3-plate Veloce
Gearbox, primary and secondary drive	
Reduction gear ratio	3.27:1
Number of gears	4
Gearbox ratios	2.078:1, 1.353:1, 1.0:1, 0.739:1
Bevel box final drive ratio	3:1
Overall gear ratios	20.4:1, 13.28:1, 9.818:1, 7.256:1
Final drive	Enclosed shaft in swing arm with UJ at rear suspension pivot
Frame, suspension and wheels	
Frame type	Tubular backbone covered with fibreglass body
Front suspension	Friction damped telescopic
Rear suspension	S/A non-adjustable
Brakes, front, diameter, width in	5 x 1
Brakes, rear, diameter, width in	5 x 1
Rim sizes	WM2 x 18 f, WM2 x 18 r
Tyre sizes	3.25 x 18 f, 3.25 x 18 r
Dimensions	
Wheelbase in	51.6
Width in	25
Seat height in	28

Velocette 200cc Vogue 1963-1968	
Unladen weight lb	275
Fuel tank capacity imp gall	2.5
Oil capacity imp pt	1.75
Gearbox capacity imp pt	0.25
Standard fuel consumption mpg	90 to 100
Top speed mph	50 to 55 at 5000rpm
Frame number	Stamped on right-hand side frame member below S/A pivot
Engine number	Stamped on crankcase, below carburettor

LE industrial engine

Introduction

During the 1960s, motorcycle sales were few, and the future of motorcycle production appeared bleak. The seasonal demand of the motorcycle market caused production and cashflow difficulties, such that Veloce Ltd was in need of another product to make, or that would provide work to relieve this situation.

The company received two inquiries to supply free-standing generator sets to power refrigerated vehicles. This seemed fortuitous as Veloce had considerable expertise by this time in the small, flat, twin LE engine, and many common parts and production tooling could be utilised in an LE-based industrial engine.

The design

It was not clear where to make the break in the unit construction LE engine to create the industrial unit. The split was made between the engine and the clutch housing, and the crankcase was redesigned to incorporate a timing chest in this area. The outer wall of the timing chest replaced the steady plate, and also served as the location for a speed governor, driven by a spur gear off the camshaft. Power output was taken from the front of the engine, with the rotor of a Dynastart acting as the flywheel.

Drawings of the crankshaft assemblies show that Veloce reverted to Mk 1 LE arrangements for bearings and lubrication. The crankshaft is supported on caged ball bearings, with large bearings adjacent to the webs at front and rear. A smaller bearing supports the front of the crank, and between the front ball bearings is the oil pump worm drive.

A notable change in the design was the

Generator powered by an LE-based industrial engine.

sump, which became a large cast iron assembly that also acted as a stand. The remaining parts were essentially LE, with the exception of the carburettor. Cooling was provided by a fan-assisted radiator the same size as that on the LE, and coolant circulation via thermal siphon was retained.

By the end of May 1966 the first prototype had been delivered, and had undergone a 1000-hour test, which proved satisfactory. Veloce, however, was unable to supply the industrial engines by the required deadline, and its customer was forced to seek out an alternative engine to fulfil immediate needs. Approximately 50 industrial engine units were supplied to A C Morrison Ltd, and fitted into ice cream vans for a customer in Australia. In this application the engine was installed in a metal box, with little air movement and inadequate coolant circulation via thermo-siphon around the cylinders. The engines failed in the Australian summer heat of 40+ degrees C, running at 3500rpm continuously under load, driving the refrigeration unit: many lasted only a few hours in these arduous conditions. The Australian customer refused to pay Morrison, which, in turn, sued Veloce for the cost of replacement – some £12,000.

Veloce contested the claim, stating it had run the engine on a dynamometer for 1000+ hours – probably true, but likely in an air temperature of 20 degrees C – so quite unrealistic for its intended use. Veloce counter-sued Morrison for £3648 for non-payment of the debt for the supply of the engines. Legal proceedings dragged on for some years until finally withdrawn in 1970, with Morrison later going into liquidation. A successful claim by Morrison could possibly have precipitated the earlier demise of Veloce Ltd, and the industrial engine saga proved very unfortunate after appearing to hold such promise.

Specials

Introduction

It is surprising to some Velocette enthusiasts that Veloce Ltd did not make a V twin engine, especially as Phil Irving was such a keen advocate of the motorcycle and sidecar, and went on to develop the Vincent range of V twins. Had his time at Veloce been extended, and had not the Second World War intervened, it is probable that Veloce could have produced a V twin under Irving's direction.

This is clearly only speculation, but many dyed-in-the-wool Velocette enthusiasts consider Veloce missed an excellent opportunity to revitalise flagging fortunes by not building a V twin. Such an engine layout was once very popular as it fitted nicely into the diamond-type bicycle frame from which motorcycles evolved, had the advantage of not being excessively wide and with torque characteristics suitable for a motorcycle and sidecar.

For use in a motorcycle frame, the V angle between the cylinders was usually reduced to around 50 degrees, which became almost standard. By comparison, Phelon and Moore

Ltd and Premiers preferred 90 degrees in their early examples; Moto Guzzi placed the cylinders at 120 degrees in 1935; JAP at 50 (60 for the 1100cc), and Anzani used 57 degrees. The overriding consideration here is one of balance. In single cylinder engines it is usual to eliminate primary out of balance forces by counterweighting the flywheel to balance the rotating parts of the big end and part of the conrod, and some element of the reciprocating parts consisting of the piston and remaining part of the conrod. This inevitably results in a primary force varying with a frequency equal to the speed of rotation, and a smaller secondary force at twice this frequency. If a second cylinder is added at 90 degrees to the first, producing a 90 degree V twin, the primary and secondary vertical forces cancel each other out, leaving a relatively insignificant secondary force of the same magnitude in vertical and horizontal planes.

Some pragmatism is usually employed in determining the included angle. Moto Guzzi adopted 120 degrees, as this was the largest angle it could achieve with a horizontal front cylinder and the rear cylinder just clearing the rear mudguard. The Vincent included angle of 47.5 degrees came about almost by chance when Phil Irving placed two Comet drawings on his drawing board, and realised that this included angle permitted the use of existing drilling jigs.

The foregoing has not prevented several dedicated enthusiasts from producing their own ideas of a Velocette V twin, however, and chief amongst these is the Vulcan, designed, manufactured and developed by Bob Higgs, a well-known engineer from the Midlands, and an active member of the Velocette Owners Club. Conceived in 1978, the Vulcan is the only V twin motorcycle based on Velocette components that has been endorsed by Veloce Ltd. The production of specials has always been an integral part of motorcycling culture, as shown in chapter 9 of *Always in the Picture* by Bob Burgess and Jeff Clew (Goose and Son, 1971). In this publication are shown a racing special consisting of a 1930 KSS engine in a 1930 KTP frame, and a vintage trials special consisting of a 1925 model AC two-stroke engine in a 1929 model U frame. Also shown are two examples of KSS engines fitted into RS frames: one, a very

The Vulcan 1000cc V twin.

standard engine belonging to Jeff Clew, and the other a KSS/KTT special constructed by Ivan Rhodes for John Muggleston. Following on from the example of Burgess and Clew, specials are also included in this book.

Bob Higgs (Vulcan designer and builder)

The Vulcan motorcycle and sidecar outfit was created by Ashby-de-la-Zouch engineer Bob Higgs. This area of England around Derby and Loughborough is remarkable for the prodigious amount of engineering talent that has developed there, particularly in respect of motorcycle engineering. This may be a result of the influence of Rolls-Royce and the Midland Railway in Derby, and Loughborough University in developing and encouraging engineering talent; well illustrated in Peter McManus' book *Derbyshire Motorcycle Maestros*. Bill Lomas, world champion and works rider for Veloce and Moto Guzzi; Dennis Jones, who constructed

several home-built, multi-cylinder racing bikes; Ted Mellors and George Silk, manufacturer of the Silk Scott, all spring to mind in this respect.

To this illustrious few can be added Bob Higgs, a modest, self-effacing gentleman, well-known in Velocette circles as the designer and constructor of the Vulcan 1000cc V twin based on M series components. What are less well known about are Bob's other achievements in developing the Velocette motorcycle.

Another very impressive project is the Higgs Special conceived to overcome some of the irritations of Velocette ownership, one of which being lack of oil tightness. Photos of the Special serve to demonstrate Bob's considerable engineering talent and understanding of Velocette motorcycles. The Higgs Special is based upon a standard RS sprung frame, but with home-built leading link forks, and many special features devised to overcome some of the less well thought out components of an MSS/Venom. Chief amongst these is the one-piece driveside crankcase and primary drive guard that houses a 12 volt alternator, although Bob also

(continues page 96)

Top: The Higgs Venom Special at Fellside.
Bottom left: The one-piece driveside crankcase and primary drive cases.
Bottom right: Details of the external oil filter (by base of downtube).

Above:
Recreation of
the Waycott
ISDT 596cc,
sohc Velocette
at Fellside
workshop.

Left:
The sidecar
chassis.

The sidecar body under development.

created an interesting design of rear-set footrests and control levers, and an external oil filter and oil circuit arrangement.

The outside primary drive case is in aluminium, as is the instrument binnacle, resulting in an extremely well thought out and constructed motorcycle, which does not have the persistent oil loss from the primary drive that is such an issue with some Velocettes.

Bob has also taken the lead, with Ivan's encouragement, in creating a replica of the Waycott ISDT 596cc SOHC sidecar outfit in the Fellside Workshop. This outfit was originally conceived by Phil Irving, and made especially for Stuart Waycott to compete against the BMW team in the 1939 ISDT. At the time of writing, this labour of love is benefiting from Bob's expertise, and steady progress is being made with the bike before work begins on reconstructing the sidecar. Prior to this project, Bob was very busy

with the Velocette Spares Company designing replacement parts and passing on his skills and expertise to Velocette riders.

The Vulcan

The Vulcan is an altogether more ambitious project from those previously described. Many consider, in light of the V twin's popularity now, that the Vulcan is the Velocette that Veloce should have made, and is, in many respects, an honorary Velocette. The following is based on an account written by Dave Minton which appeared in *The Classic Motor Cycle* in January 1985. Work began on the Vulcan in 1982; the concept was to take over where Charles Udall, Phil Irving and the Goodmans had left off, as Bob Higgs created an integrated sidecar outfit that would have pleased Phil Irving. To this end the sidecar is an integral part of the whole, although it carries a Steib S501 sidecar body, and the fuel tank is slung under the sidecar frame, with a pump supplying a small header tank above the engine to feed the carburettors. The traditional fuel tank is a fibreglass dummy that covers the engine. A car alternator of 180W capacity is driven direct end-on from the crankshaft. The frame is based on standard Veloce geometry with a steering head angle of 63 degrees. It is a full cradle type, with the front having been fabricated by Bob. The rear parts are standard RS but with strengthened rear swing arm pivot mountings.

The wheelbase is 2.75 inches (69.8mm) longer than a standard Velocette of 53.75 inches (1.365mm) to accommodate the 60-degree V twin engine. This dimension was arrived at through a compromise of retaining a Velocette appearance whilst keeping the wheelbase within reasonable limits. Ideally, a 90 degree included V angle would have been preferred from the point of view of balance, but this would have caused other problems.

Designing the crankcases and producing the outline and detail drawings took some four months of Bob's spare time. The castings were made locally and given thick walls to accommodate the additional loading they were expected to carry. The crankshaft flywheel is based on MSS; a balance factor of 42 per cent was initially achieved by rim drilling, but this was later improved to 50 per cent. The 1-inch (25.4mm) diameter mainshafts were retained, but the taper roller main bearings have an increased outer cage diameter of 2.7 inches (68.5mm) to reduce crankcase loading, which is also assisted by a steel plate on the driveside. The bearings have a six thou nip when set up. The connecting rod big ends run side-by-side on an extra-long crank pin that has a shrunk-on bronze collar to separate the big ends. The 1-inch (25.4mm) cylinder offset assists in cooling the rear cylinder. The cam drive is standard Velocette for each cylinder, with the cylinder offset accommodated by bolting together two idler pinions for the rear cylinder.

One idler is driven by the crankshaft pinion and the other drives the cam wheel. Solid skirt Omega pistons to Clubman specification fill the bores, which have $1/16$ inch (1.5mm) packing

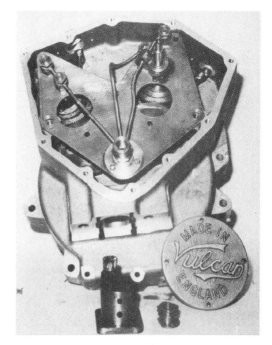

Top: High stability at speed is delivered by a long wheelbase and Higgs-made leading link forks.

Centre: The flywheel assembly drilled for balance.

Left: crankcases with oil pump and oil lines to the timing gears.

at the crankcase. The oil pump is standard Velocette, but with a three-start worm gear to increase feed rate from a six pint (3.3l) tank by 50 per cent. Drive chains are standard size MSS and have managed well with the extra load, but the standard MSS clutch found it difficult to cope with the degree of torque produced by the engine.

Since 1984 the Vulcan has been subjected to continuous development; in many ways it is a rolling test and development bed. The monobloc carburettors have been replaced with Amal Mk 1.5 concentrics of 28mm choke. The standard Velocette front hub and brake have been replaced by a 7R backplate and shoes operating in an aluminium alloy hub copied from an AJS design. The rear hub is standard full width Velocette. The rear brake was initially

*A proud owner
at one with his
creation.*

standard Velocette but is now hydraulic, utilising BMC Mini components within the brake drum, coupled to a standard Steib sidecar brake. The 19-inch front wheel accommodates a 3.25 x 19in tyre and the rear wheel a 4 x 18in. The sidecar has a 16in diameter wheel. All wheels have alloy rims.

The clutch has required the major part of the development work, and variations of its design have included an all-metal, wet, multi-plate (steel bronze) unit of Bob's design running in automatic transmission fluid. This worked well but the hydraulic fluid could not be kept in the chain case, and was not suitable for the cush drive. Very heavy springs were required in this configuration. This clutch was replaced with a version of the Velocette design that comprises six steel and six bronze plates in a deepened chain wheel, itself fitted with square bronze inserts. These clutch plates were all drilled and angularly slotted opposite the tongues to prevent them 'dishing.'

The current clutch design comprises ordinary Veloce-style plain steel and segmented friction plates – eleven in total.

The central spring holder has 20 springs and the clutch backplate has been modified to accept six rollers for a smoother peel-off. The hinged thrust cup releasing mechanism has been strengthened to reduce bending, and the internal bellcrank and plunger rod system has been replaced with a hydraulic unit. There is little lift available in a multi-plate Velo clutch, so a hydraulic actuation is used to reduce lost motion.

The quality of workmanship that Bob is able to achieve is remarkable. The fibreglass is all his own work, produced by using chicken wire and masking tape formers instead of plaster moulds, as this saved time and money. All paintwork is stove-enamelled. The gearchange lever is a work of art that folds away to allow operation of the kick-start, often to the bewilderment of onlookers.

The outfit can cruise happily at 70mph, and can reach a maximum speed of around 95mph. In the 40 years since it was created the Vulcan has travelled many thousands of miles, often covering hundreds of miles on the VOC Peaks run.

Table 3.9 Vulcan specifications

Vulcan 1982	
Type of engine	Four-stroke V twin OHV
Cylinders	60 degree V twin, 86 x 86mm, capacity 998cc
Compression ratio	8.4:1
Output bhp	Not known
Valve system	OHV, pushrod
Ignition	Coil ignition with 12 volt Lucas 180W alternator
Engine lubrication system	Dry sump, gear oil pump
Carburettor	2 Amal monobloc type 363/Mk 1 concentric
Clutch	Mk 5, 12 slotted plate, 6 steel and 6 bronze
Gearbox, primary and secondary drive	
Reduction gear ratio	3.27:1
Number of gears	4, MSS prefix 14 internals
Gearbox ratios	2.52:1, 1.75:1, 1.206:1, 1:1
Overall gear ratios (sidecar) :1	10.75, 7.43, 5.65, 4.25
Primary drive	$1/2$ x $5/16$ chain
Final drive	$3/8$ x $5/8$ chain
Frame, suspension and wheels	
Frame type	Duplex cradle
Front suspension	Leading link 1½ inch trail
Rear suspension	S/A, adjustable for load (Irving patent)
Brakes, front	Copy of AJS hub with 7R backplate, internal expanding
Brakes, rear	Hydraulic coupled to sidecar, Velocette drum with BMC internals
Wheel rim sizes, rear, front	WM2 x 18 f, WM2 x 19 r
Tyre sizes, rear, front	400 x 18 f, 325 x 19 r
Sidecar wheel in	16
Wheelbase in	56.5
Fuel tank capacity imp gall	3.0
Oil tank capacity imp pt	6
Top speed mph	90 to 95

Overview

Chapter 4

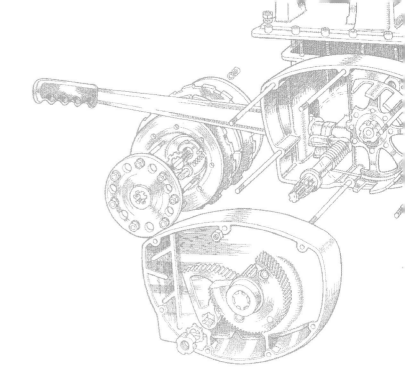

Towards the end of WW2 the directors of Veloce conducted a market survey, and concluded that the time was right for the production of the oft-considered 'motorcycle for everyman': an inexpensive, but not cheap, quality motorcycle, to cater to an expected post-war demand for personal mobility.

It was envisaged that post-war austerity would limit sales of the 'superbike' Model O, and, as it turned out, the Roarer was never raced, as supercharging in road racing was banned by the FIM. When motorcycle production resumed in 1947, only the M series and KSS were listed, but 1948 proved to be the MOV, MSS and KSS models' swan song because, from 1949, only the MAC model remained in production, as all efforts were focused on bringing the LE to production.

The LE made its debut during 1948 and took the motorcycling world by surprise, as it was unlike any previous Veloce design. Such were the expectations that Veloce had for the LE it was anticipated that even the MAC would be phased out when orders for the LE materialised.

In anticipation of large orders, a moving track assembly line was constructed in the factory with a production target of 300 machines per week: a very ambitious figure, considering that the previous best weekly output of singles had been 118 machines. Alas, the public – fickle as ever – did not buy the LE in the numbers anticipated by Veloce senior management, and the subsequent highest number of machines produced in one week was 169. Production of 120 LEs in a week could be regularly achieved, but this was often interrupted when production of the singles was resumed to compensate for disappointing LE sales.

A considerable boost to LE production occurred when several orders were received from police forces, as the LE proved a useful machine for local patrols that could be used virtually 24 hours a day, with lengthy maintenance intervals. It is most likely that these orders, being of large volume, would have been heavily discounted, not generating much profit for the company, but they did serve to bring the machine to public attention and led to some design improvements, especially in the electrical and lighting areas.

It's interesting to consider what may have happened had not external forces conspired against Veloce in development of the Twins. Would the Roarer have been the success that was anticipated? Probably not, is the opinion of Phil Irving. Two main factors were against it; the first was weight. The added complexity of two crankshafts meant the machine weighed-in at a hefty 375lb, even though the frame was lighter than that of the standard Mk 8 KTT, owing to the use of all-welded joints rather than malleable lugs pinned and brazed. The TT-winning supercharged BMW of 1939 weighed just 300lb by comparison. The steel tank was heavy – as weighty as a full modern aluminium tank – but, this apart, there is little scope for weight reduction elsewhere.

The second factor of concern was that of cooling. Supercharging is intended to increase the specific output of an engine, which inevitably increases the cooling load. In the original layout drawings of 1937, liquid cooling was detailed, but the policy of the factory to make the racing bikes outwardly similar to production bikes led to air cooling being adopted at a late stage in the initial design process. This is difficult to understand, considering the lengths Willis had gone to in producing the Huntley and Palmer head to ensure adequate cooling on the KTT. The main problem was ensuring adequate cooling around the exhaust valves which, in 1939, were relatively weak when hot, such that a dropped valve head was not uncommon. The air scoops fitted to the side of the engine as an afterthought were intended to direct air around the rear of the engine, but it's unlikely that these were very effective. This was probably a catastrophic error as, by the time this decision had been made, other factors – such as location of the compressor and rear-facing exhausts – had been decided upon.

It has been said that Willis was put off liquid cooling when he saw the large radiator on the V4 AJS, not realising that only half was actually in use. This is an extraordinary statement because several heat exchanger manufacturers in Birmingham were producing specialised heat exchangers for the aircraft industry at that time, and could have been approached for advice.

Had the Roarer been developed, it's likely that a solution could have been found by adopting a practice developed by Tatra – used on its two-cylinder T607 and eight-cylinder T603 engines – that of exhaust gas ejector cooling.

In this, the energy of the exhaust gases is used to create low pressure in the region of the exhaust pipes to draw cooling air over the engine. Such devices are self-regulating, very responsive, and mechanically very reliable.

It has been said that development of the Roarer was curtailed post-war by the FIM ban on supercharging, but there must have been other factors to consider, as an examination of the engine drawings show that the supercharger could have been removed and the head rotated around the camshaft drive to bring the exhausts to the front of the engine. The now naturally-aspirated engine would have required changes in valve sizes and cam profile, perhaps to Mk 8 components to get the best out of it, but this would not have been problematic.

It is difficult today, when a formula GP or Formula I racing team requires tens of millions of pounds to participate each year, to understand how a small family firm such as Veloce could consider producing a world-beating racing bike as sophisticated as the Roarer, and alongside it the production version, the Model O. The Model O was arguably the first 'superbike' developed by any manufacturer, and offered a level of performance and sophistication then unknown in a motorcycle. To say the Model O was mothballed when development of the Roarer was stopped is possibly not the complete story: it's more likely that Veloce considered a period of post-war austerity was not the best time to produce a machine that inevitably would be a luxury bike, appealing to a small market. Perhaps suggestions of a demand for personal transport following the cessation of hostilities, as happened after the Great War, led Veloce to develop the 'everyman' motorcycle. Not foreseen or anticipated was development of the small motor car, or introduction of supermarkets and the changes in behaviour that these would bring. The LE-mounted housewife would no longer shop daily at the local butcher or baker, preferring to carry her weekly shop in a Mini or Escort.

Certainly, Veloce was fascinated by the LE, an in-house design demonstrating the ingenuity of its engineering, likely looked on more favourably than the Irving-designed Model O. If there had been any arguments over which bike to produce, Irving wasn't around to fight his corner; a pity as the Model O was designed by a very talented engineer with production in mind. Following initial development problems it proved to be, and is, very smooth, fast and reliable, and would have been a welcome addition to the very popular vertical twin-cylinder sector of the market.

The LE was a fundamentally new design but was not plucked out of the air in a complete form. Engineers build on what they know, and the LE clearly drew on the ideas and technology developed in the Roarer and Model O. Table 4.1 indicates the common elements that the LE shares with other Veloce twins, from which

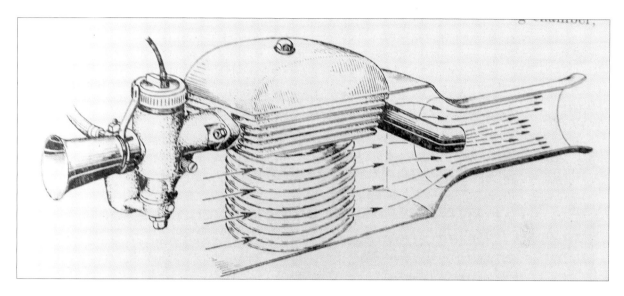

it can be seen that the LE has more in common with the Roarer than the Model O. Some of the common elements would have been dictated by company policy: for instance, contra-rotating masses and shaft drive stem from the original specification of the Roarer as laid out by Willis. The use of pressed steel body parts on the LE must also have been determined by company policy to make use of the presses purchased when the Model O was being conceived. Other elements, however, come from the preference of the designer and, as the Roarer and the LE both came off Udall's drawing board, it's not surprising that they have similar elements.

Charles Udall clearly felt that his shaft drive design, enclosed within the swing arm that acted as a torque tube, was superior to Phil Irving's exposed driveshaft on the Model O, but he saw the benefit of the adjustable suspension patented jointly by Irving and Veloce that was employed on the Model O, and the subsequent RS sprung frame of the M series bikes. The integrated drivetrain, later reinvented by BMW for the K series, clearly had advantages with regard to volume production of the LE. This was an improved version of that designed for the Roarer, as it used the engine and gearbox as a frame member with fixing points at the front and rear. This allowed the bottom rails of the Roarer frame to be dispensed with, thus making removal of the LE body quite straightforward, especially when the bottom rail of the front tubular frame member was made detachable.

Table 4.1 Design elements common to the Roarer, Model O and LE

Element	Roarer	Model O	LE
Contra-rotating masses	X	X	X
Shaft drive	X	X	X
Driveshaft enclosed in swinging arm	X		X
Integrated drive system	X		X
Crankshaft centre line below wheel spindle centre line	X		X
All-indirect gears	X		X
Multi-plate clutch	X		X
Pressed steel body		X	X
Adjustable rear suspension		X	X
Wet sump		X	X

The Roarer and Model O clutches are quite different. Irving had in mind to use car components for low cost and ease of maintenance when he laid out the Model O. Consequently, his clutch – initially a single plate later changed to two – is of large diameter, being located on the starboardside flywheel and actuated by a rocking thrust plate. The Roarer clutch is a small diameter multi-plate device, located with its own backplate in a chamber aft of and connected to the coupling gear on the engine portside. The driving member of the clutch carries ten shouldered studs, on which are 20 small diameter coil springs and the driving plates. The driven plates are located on a hollow splined

Schematic illustration of exhaust-driven ejector cooling.

shaft that engages with the gearbox input shaft, which is also hollow. When assembled, the clutch plates are together compressed against the spring pressure by nuts pulled up against the shoulders on the studs. The first driving plate carries a thrust button at the centre that, when pressed by a rod running through the hollow shafts, is forced against the springs and the friction force released. The LE clutch is identical in form and operation except that, on their outer edges, the driven plates engage with a bell connected to the gearbox input shaft. The clutch design is very unorthodox by motorcycle standards, and a good example of Charles Udall's clever and original approach to solving engineering problems.

The Model O utilised MOV gear components, which required that the output shaft was at the same height as the input shaft, setting the engine high in the frame. This allowed room for a deep wet sump below the engine that followed car engine practice, yet still allowed sufficient ground clearance for cornering. The Roarer, however, was designed to be an out-and-out racer, so, in this case, the engine was set as low in the frame as possible without compromising handling. It was then necessary to raise the gearbox output shaft in line with the bevel box to minimise angling of the driveshaft. This was achieved by using large diameter gears,

all-indirect, with the gear ratios shared by the gearbox and the bevel box.

In the case of the LE an indirect box is the only way of transmitting drive from the input on the centre line of the bike to the line of the output, be it chain or shaft. Once the decision to have an inline crankshaft was taken, an indirect gearbox naturally followed. The LE engine is so small, however, that there is ample room to fit a pressed steel sump below the engine, and the space under the raised gearbox is perfect for a box silencer.

It is evident that the LE shared much of its detail work with the Roarer, which isn't surprising as they came off the same drawing board. Once the basic specification had been decided, and the decision to use pressed steel body parts had been made, the details were very much up to the design team. Had Phil Irving been able to take his designs of the LE to completion it would have been a quite different machine to that of Charles Udall. Much has been said regarding the LE being the cause of the demise of Veloce; undoubtedly mistakes were made, and this view is open to conjecture, but there is no doubt in the author's mind that the LE, from an engineering point of view, is the finest lightweight motorcycle ever made by any manufacturer, and it can and should be held in the same regard as the Roarer and the Model O.

Postscript

Chapter 5

Veloce has always had a reputation for producing racing motorcycles, be they factory specials for the works rider or replicas (KTTs) for the general public. Post-war, KTT production ceased, though the race shop was still busy providing machines for Freddie Frith and Bob Foster to become 350cc World Champions in 1949 and 1950 respectively. The race team was supported by Lincolnshire jam manufacturer Nigel Spring, using a new DOHC engine designed and developed by Bertie Goodman alongside a pre-war SOHC engine on some circuits.

This arrangement continued in 1951 with Bill Lomas, Bob Foster and Cecil Sandford riding a full range of 250, 350 and 500cc machines. Unfortunately, these bikes suffered unreliability issues, possibly brought about by the need to focus on LE production difficulties in the factory. Veloce was famous for its overhead camshaft (OHC) KTT single, which was a completely reliable, world-beating 350, yet victory in the Senior TT had always eluded the marque, and, however satisfying it might be to win the Junior race, there was not the same glamour or kudos as with success in the major capacity class. Perhaps, after all, it was time to turn away from the traditional single …

Thoughts turned to resurrecting the Roarer by rotating the head through 180 degrees, bringing the exhaust pipes to the front and dispensing with the supercharger. The problem was placed in the hands of Percy Goodman, who began to sketch a possible power unit. Like the

pre-war twin, this had separate, contra-rotating crankshafts parallel to the frame axis to facilitate the use of shaft drive, and cancel out torque reaction: it would have water cooling as preferred by Phil Irving.

Yet even before the general arrangement drawing of the revived twin was completed, still more exciting possibilities were being considered. A four with small cylinders offered the potential for more power and would fit neatly across a frame. The updated Roarer was put to one side and the decision taken to go ahead with the design, not only of the four-cylinder power unit but also of the necessary cycle parts.

By 1951 the initial layout was ready, and development of the detail drawings was put in the hands of motorcycle designer and engineer G H Jones, with a view to having the bike ready for the 1953 TT. Jones was approached by Percy Goodman at the Earls Court Show, and offered the opportunity to complete the detail drawings from the layout sketches produced by Percy. Working late into the night at home, and with frequent journeys to Hall Green, Jones completed the job in a year.

The entire project was shrouded in the tightest secrecy. Apart from Jones and the Veloce directors, hardly anyone knew what was going on. Basic layout was for an across the frame, vertical, inline design; the crankshaft coupled to the gearbox by intermediate gears and bevels, and final drive by shaft. The gearbox was inline with the frame.

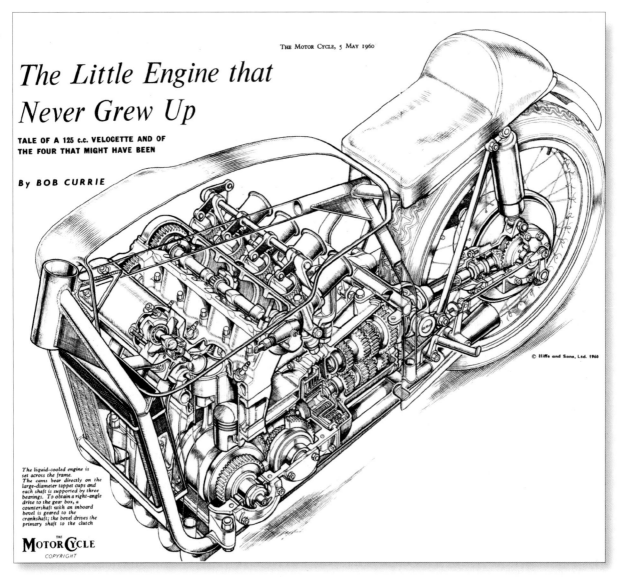

THE MOTOR CYCLE, 5 MAY 1960

The Little Engine that Never Grew Up

TALE OF A 125 c.c. VELOCETTE AND OF THE FOUR THAT MIGHT HAVE BEEN

By BOB CURRIE

The liquid-cooled engine is set across the frame. The cams bear directly on the large-diameter tappet cups and each shaft is supported by three bearings. To obtain a right-angle drive to the gear box, a countershaft with an inboard bevel is geared to the crankshaft; the bevel drives the primary shaft to the clutch

THE MOTOR CYCLE
COPYRIGHT

© Iliffe and Sons, Ltd. 1960

Schematic of the four-cylinder engine. (Courtesy The Motorcycle)

Unlike the Gilera and MV fours, the Veloce machine was water-cooled, and the hoped for power output was 55-60bhp (41–44 kW). The two overhead camshafts were driven by a train of gears, and the cams worked on hardened followers at the top of each valve stem. Each cylinder had a single 10mm sparkplug, and the sparks were to be provided by a Lucas racing magneto. The crank was built up so that roller big ends and mains could be used, and there was no flywheel: the reason for this was mainly a manufacturing one as it would have been difficult in the extreme to incorporate a central flywheel,

whilst an outside flywheel would have imposed too much stress on the crank.

Percy was in failing health and so Bertie took over, finishing the work in 1952 and putting in hand construction of an experimental 125cc engine, from which test-bench data was to be acquired.

The 125cc single was virtually the right-hand cylinder of the projected four, complete with full-scale drive to the overhead camshafts. If 15bhp could be produced from the single, then, theoretically, approximately 60bhp (44kW) would be available from the completed engine.

Unfortunately, just before the experimental unit was ready for testing, Percy Goodman died, and the company decided to withdraw from racing, which could no longer be justified as an economical form of advertising. The four design remained in the Veloce archives and was described by Bertie Goodman in an article published in *Motorcycling* (Feb 6, 1965 pages 8-9) that discussed a proposal to build a British 500cc racing motorcycle funded by the Isle of Man lottery –

"The preliminary work on it was already completed at the Velocette factory. It is a liquid-cooled four. All the detailed drawings have been done, and that alone represents a saving of up to £2000. Things have gone even further with a 125cc unit – effectively, one quarter of the complete engine – for bench development work. For this 'pilot rig,' all the pattern equipment and some castings have been made – another £3-4000 worth of work already done.

"Why the choice of a four by a factory already making four-stroke singles and twins and a two-stroke twin? Let's look at the alternatives we had to consider. A single? No. Super-tuning to reach the absolute ceiling of 'Venom' performance would not fill the bill, though, as all providers of TT works machinery know so well, £20,000 or more can be whittled away in a season or two of simply extracting a couple more bhp from an old design. True, the single is still responsive to further development, but we are very near to the limits of piston speed, and the necessarily great distance from the centre of the piston to the cylinder wall slows down heat dissipation. And torque is not smooth because of the relatively long period between firing strokes. So the single is out. Then what about twins in their various forms? Our experience is that the conventional vertical twin on a common crankshaft creates a bad 'couple,' and, for other reasons, is an engine rather seriously out of balance. Consequently, excessive vibration has to be absorbed by using a heavier than necessary frame.

"Far better balance is obtained in the vertical twin with two crankshafts geared together: in effect, two single engines running in opposite directions. This was the layout used on the 1939 Velocette 'Roarer,' which was ridden in practice for the 1939 TT but never raced because war prevented all further development (and supercharging, for which it was designed, was banned by the FIM after the war). The geared twin is heavier than its single crankshaft equivalent, but, thanks to its smoothness, can be carried in a lighter frame. The horizontally-opposed twin is an extremely smooth engine, but if its crankshaft is parallel to the frame axis, it gives a torque reaction that impairs machine handling as a whole, while, if the shaft lies across the frame, it is difficult to accommodate the gearbox.

"Finally, all large capacity twins share, though to a lesser extent, two of the problems of the single: the distance from the centre of the piston is a little too great for maximum heat dissipation, and more than two valves per cylinder may become necessary for effective breathing. If twins are rejected, there remains the engine of four or more cylinders, if it is to be a four-stroke, and that is the type of unit with which my company has the greatest experience.

"More than four cylinders introduces costly complications, so a four it should be. And that is the line of thinking which led Veloce, logically, as long ago as 1950, to start planning this inline four of 54.1mm bore and stroke (495cc). The unit is set across the frame, but the frontal area of a liquid-cooled four is not detrimental. Using wet liners permits the cylinders to be grouped more closely than if they were air-cooled. Total width of the unit is, in fact, about 14.1 inches, and the radiator is even narrower.

"A vane-type pump circulates coolant through a pressurised system, which permits a small radiator to be used: the pressure raising the operating temperature of the coolant, of course.

"Other advantages of liquid cooling are even temperature control, eliminating hot spots and distortion, and the ready availability of the right sort of cooling for supercharging, should it be adopted later.

"Valve operation is by twin camshafts acting through thimble-type tappets on to the eight valve stems; the drive being by spur gears from the nearside of the crankshaft.

"10mm sparkplugs are thought to be best in order to obtain a spark point as near as possible to the centre of the hemispherical combustion chamber, and so derive optimum power. The crankshaft of the prototype is of pressed-up construction, allowing the use of caged roller bearing big ends and centre roller main bearings.

"Transmission layout is governed by the

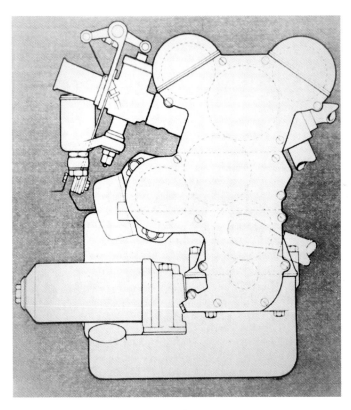

Outline of the four-cylinder engine.

decision to use shaft final drive, which, unlike a chain, maintains efficiency constantly throughout a long race, as well as reducing the risk of oil being flung onto the tyre.

"To provide direct drive to the shaft, the gearbox, which can house five or six gears, is set parallel to the frame axis. Power is taken off the nearside main shaft, and the drive turned through 90 degrees by bevel gears to a conventional multi-plate clutch mounted in front of the box.

"The driving bevel is, in fact, on a countershaft and faces inwards to bring the clutch centre-line further inboard.

The choice of five or six speeds would depend on the finalised characteristics of the engine: if a wide power range is forthcoming, then five speeds will suffice. But, in either case, in order to reduce power loss, lubrication is by jet feed from the engine, which maintains a film of oil on the gears in a 'dry' box.

"Considerable development work would, of course, be necessary; it is here, in particular, that large sums of money can be spent.

"There is undoubtedly room for experiment

in fuel injection, with its theoretical advantages, but, for the time being, I would stick to the well-proven carburettor, with one per cylinder. Transistorised ignition, currently used on Grand Prix racing cars, will eliminate magneto drive power loss, and be more efficient than coil ignition at high speeds.

"My company has experimented with rotary valves of two different types – in both cases on four-stroke engines – without deriving any benefit. Though it may be feasible for rotary valves, with improved sealing, to be used in the future one would have neither time nor money to devote to development of this nature.

"The four can, of course, be considered as a multiple of 125cc. If in the future an attack on the 125 and 250cc classes should be envisaged, then here would be a ready-made single or twin of the appropriate size and potency. In any case, to reduce cost, development work on the four would be carried out on a single 125cc component, consisting essentially of the timing side of the four-cylinder engine.

"Indeed, one of these 125s was put in hand by my company, and nearly completed before our withdrawal from racing in 1952. Another two weeks of finished machining work, and it could be running ... Maximum use would be made of modern materials such as titanium and magnesium. The frame – drawings for which have also been completed – is of duplex construction, with bottom leading link front forks, swinging fork rear suspension; hydraulically-operated disc brakes at the front, and conventional drum-type cable-operated rear brake. The complete machine should scale at 300-325lb when carrying approximately four pints of coolant and six pints of oil. The engine should develop between 70 and 75bhp at 12,000rpm, giving the machine a maximum speed of approximately 170-175mph when fitted with a dolphin-type fairing.

"Would this be a world-beater? I think it would."

At the factory closure parts for the single-cylinder test engine passed into the hands of Ralph Seymour, who put them on display in the Hawthorn works. They still exist, and are now in the hands of a Veloce enthusiast.

Recently, the drawings of the Velocette four produced by Bertie have been rediscovered and are being preserved. Does this bode well for the creation of a Velocette 4, as has been done with the Roarer by Dan Smith in Vancouver (www.motorcycleclassics.com 'The Birmingham Blower')? Using modern computer-aided manufacturing, 3D printing techniques and additive manufacturing will simplify the production of castings, and modern fuel injection and ignition systems also reduce design complexity.

What of the LE ... was it an impossible dream ... an act of faith by a manufacturer who wanted to provide the very best means of transport to an unappreciative public? Was the LE responsible for the demise of the company?

This is difficult to say. Certainly by the 1960s, interest in motorcycles had declined in Britain, and by 1964, most LEs were built for the police, although a few were still sold to the general public. As already noted, it's likely that police orders were heavily discounted and so returned little profit, which would not have helped the financial viability of the company: already very bad in the late 1960s following misguided ventures into the scooter market and industrial engine production. It is doubtful that sales of the Valiant and Vogue covered their tooling costs.

It is very sad that such a sophisticated bike as the LE was so fatally flawed at conception; to quote Titch Allen: "The LE had the price and sophistication of a Rolls-Royce with the performance of an Austin Seven."

On the face of it, that a small firm like Veloce was so successful in motorcycle production and racing, when competing with larger UK companies and other concerns whose owners had very deep pockets and good income from other products, is surprising. Even in its most successful years, Veloce had to balance the books and show restraint with some of its commitments. Producing a bespoke quality product in a competitive market in limited numbers for a dedicated enthusiast is not an easy task. Perhaps the most remarkable factor is that such a wealth of talent migrated to the Veloce works, and Veloce it was who led the way with so many innovations for others to follow. Had Veloce been located in Italy rather than the UK there is no doubt that a statue to Percy Goodman, who did so much for British prestige, would have been erected similar to that paying homage to Carlo Guzzi in Mandello del Lario on Lake Como.

Disappointing sales of the LE, Valiant and

Vogue forced Veloce to continue production of the well-established single-cylinder range based upon the MOV of Eugene Goodman. The MAC engine was redesigned in 1953, with an aluminium head incorporating fully enclosed valves, and fitted in a new swinging arm frame (RS) based on the race-proven geometry of the KTT. The 500cc engine was then redesigned by Charles Udall, with square 86 x 86 bore and stroke to fit into the new RS frame. The first model with this engine, the MSS, appeared in 1954, and the unit went on in different guises to power a range of bikes from the 1955 Scrambler to the Sports Venom and 350cc Viper. On 18-19 March, 1961 a carefully-prepared Venom set a world 24-hour record for a 500cc motorcycle of 100.05mph. At the time of writing the record still stands. This then led to development of the Thruxton production racer of 1965 that, ridden by Neil Kelly, won the inaugural production TT in 1971.

These bikes were well received by enthusiasts because of their build quality and strong performance, but in spite of having a too wide range of models, Veloce directors decided to venture into the scooter market to boost sales. In hindsight this was ill advised as this market – very buoyant in the 1950s – had peaked, as small cars such as the Mini were becoming more affordable.

Veloce's idea of what constituted a scooter was announced in 1960 as the Viceroy. This was built to exacting Veloce standards with large wheels, properly damped suspension, and perfect weight distribution that contributed to very stable roadholding and handling. The large pressed steel body was placed on a step-through backbone frame that offered excellent weather protection. Veloce developed a new horizontally-opposed two-cylinder two-stroke engine of 54mm bore and stroke producing a swept volume of 247cc. Induction was via a single carburettor and reed valves, and, as both cylinders fired together, it had an unusual sound for a two-stroke. The engine unit was placed at the front of the backbone frame in front of the feet of the rider, connected to a combined swing arm and transmission unit by a propeller shaft. The transmission and swing arm unit was based upon LE components. It contained a chain-driven primary reduction to the clutch basket, the clutch and gear cluster, bevel box and rear brake in a

Line drawing of the Viceroy scooter.

light alloy casting that pivoted on large bushes located at the front. The front forks were based on LE units.

Unfortunately, the Viceroy was not a success; in total, 697 complete machines found buyers, and a small number of engines were sold to DMW to power the Deemster. The Viceroy was listed in the 1965 Veloce catalogue but no new machines were manufactured after 1964. So came to an end the last complete design from Veloce Ltd.

The company struggled on for a few more years with diminishing sales and the high cost of producing a bespoke motorcycle. The situation was eased when an agreement was made with the Enfield Cycle Company of Redditch to service

and sell the Royal Enfield spares range, but the inevitable could not be held off indefinitely. By the end of 1970 the liabilities of the company were on the point of exceeding its assets. The family, true to its usual honesty and integrity, called in the Receiver and Veloce Ltd went into voluntary liquidation on February 4, 1971. All of the company's creditors were paid in full, 20 shillings in the pound.

Not long after the factory closed the premises were demolished to make way for new development, bringing to a complete end a company whose quality and technical excellence was reflected in the integrity and honesty of purpose of the machines it produced.

VELOCE LIMITED *(in liquidation)* P.O. Box No. 275, Hall Green Works, York Road, Hall Green, Birmingham B28 8LN

Velocette

Telephone: 021-777 1145
Private Branch Exchange
Telegrams: Veloce, Birmingham
Codes, Bentley's

VELOCETTE MOTOR CYCLES

Royal Enfield Spares & Service Division
General Engineers & Suppliers of Petrol Engines

Your Reference

Our Reference

4th February, 1971.

N O T I C E

With effect from Friday, February 5th 1971,
the main gates to the works will be locked, and
all employees should enter and leave via the
office entrance.

No vehicles will be allowed past the gates,
and the car park should be used.

....
Liquidator

Notice from the liquidator advising the closure of Veloce Ltd.

Bibliography

A Classic World & When the Engine Roars, G Begg, Begg and Allen Ltd, 1999

Always in the Picture: History of the Velocette Motorcycle, R W Burgess, J R Clew, Goose and Son, 1971

Bill Lomas, World Champion Road Racer, Bill Lomas, Redline Books, 2002

Classic Motorcycle Engines, Vic Willoughby, MRP, 2000

Classic Motorcycles, Vic Willoughby, Hamlyn, 1975

Derbyshire Motorcycling Maestros, Peter McManus, MEP Publishers, 2013

From the Race Shop Floor, H J Cox, Xlibris, 2009

Motorcycle Engineering, P E Irving, Clymer Publications, 1973

My Velocette Days, L Moseley, Transport Bookman Publications, 1974

Norm's Technicalities, N Trig, Velocette Owners Club Australia (Inc) Edition, 2009

Past Masters of Speed, D May, Temple Press Ltd, 1958

Phil Irving – An Autobiography, P E Irving, Turton and Armstrong, Sydney, 1992

The First Velocette Scene, B Main-Smith, BMS Publications, 1977

The Racing Motor Cycle, Vic Willoughby, Hamlyn, 1980

The Story of the Velocette, G Beresford, G S Davison, 1950

The Velocette Saga, C Edgar Allen, Amulree Publications, 1994

Tuning for Speed, Slide Rule, P E Irving, Temple Press Ltd, 1949

Velocette – Passion of a Lifetime, I Rhodes (self-published)

Velocette Flat Twins, R Bacon, Osprey Collector's Library, 1985

Velocette Race Shop Memoirs, Check No 134 Veloce Ltd (Frank Panes), VOC, 2002

Velocette: Technical Excellence Exemplified, I Rhodes, Osprey Collectors Library, 1990

Appendix

Clubs

The Velocette Owners Club

The Velocette Owners Club was formed in 1957 at a pub called The Red House, which used to be located at St John's Wood. The club has now grown to 28 UK centres with several overseas centres. Velocettes have always attracted riders who possess a modicum of engineering competence, and who appreciate quality motorcycles. Following closure of the factory the club has been the main focus for Velocette activities, and it has formed a company called Veloce Spares Ltd to provide difficult to obtain parts not available elsewhere. The club has approximately 2500 members, who all receive a magazine entitled *Fishtail* that presents the latest club news, reports of events, in-depth technical articles, history, and, of course, the good ol' days. It comes out eight times a year and always carries a number of opportunities to find parts and bikes, and to sell and exchange stuff, too, all free to members.

The web address for the club is:
https://www.velocetteowners.com/

The LE Velo Club

Formed in the early summer of 1950 from a spontaneous rally of riders meeting at Newlands Corner, just outside Guildford in Surrey, the LE Velo Club has survived the changing values of more than six decades. Now into its 7th decade, it has over 1300 members worldwide, and is a limited company committed to promoting the enjoyment, riding and restoration of the post-war lightweight models: the LE, Vogue, Valiant and Viceroy. The club has an extensive parts department providing members with new and used parts to keep their machines alive, as well as a monthly magazine and other benefits.

https://www.le-velo-club.com

More great books from Veloce Publishing:

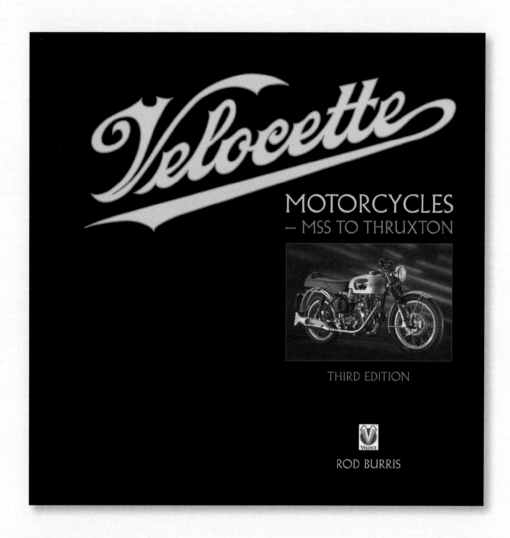

The definitive development history of the most famous Velocette
motorcycles, this third edition includes updated information and very
comprehensive appendices about this historic marque.

ISBN: 978-1-787112-48-3
Paperback • 22.5x22.5cm • 224 pages
• 450 colour and b&w pictures

**For more information and price details, visit our website at
www.veloce.co.uk
email: info@veloce.co.uk • Tel: +44(0)1305 260068**

How to buy a secondhand Velocette single – this book covers the various models available, what to check and problem points to look out for, plus investment potential, specifications and useful contacts.

ISBN: 978-1-845849-41-2
Paperback • 19.5x13.9cm • 64 pages
• 100 pictures

More in the Essential Buyer's Guide series:

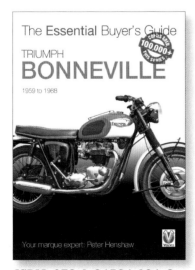

ISBN: 978-1-84584-134-8

ISBN: 978-1-787116-06-1

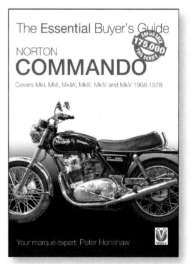

ISBN: 978-1-787116-52-8

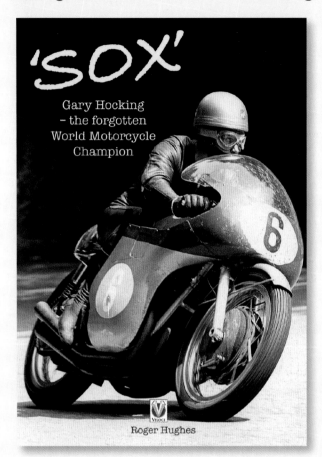
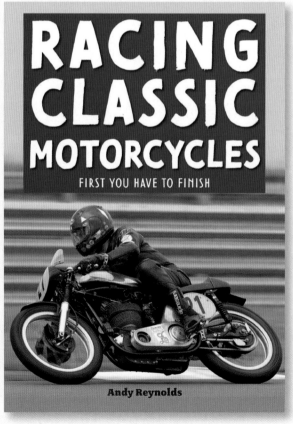

Motorcycling social history, as seen from the saddle. Bill Snelling's entertaining autobiography recounts a lifetime spent at the heart of British motorcycle sport, and living on the Isle of Man.

ISBN: 978-1-787115-81-1
Paperback • 21x14.8cm • 160 pages • 202 pictures

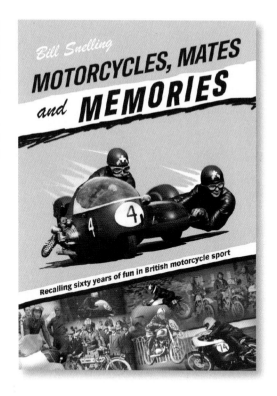

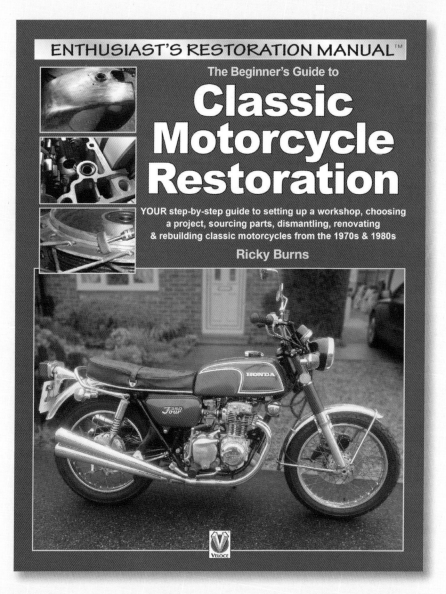

Index